Looking and Writing

Looking and Writing
A Guide for Art History Students

Marilyn Wyman
San Jose State University

Upper Saddle River, NJ 07458

Library of Congress Cataloging-in-Publication Data

Wyman, Marilyn.
    Looking and writing : a guide for art history students / Marilyn Wyman.
        p.   cm.
    Includes index.
    ISBN 0-13-098359-4
        1. Art—History—Handbooks, manuals, etc.   2. Art—Authorship—Handbooks,
    manuals, etc.   3. Report writing—Handbooks, manuals, etc.   4. Art—Information
    resources—Handbooks, manuals, etc.   I. Title.
N5303   .W97   2003
701'.18—dc21

2002022425

Publisher: *Bud Therien*
Production editor: *Laura A. Lawrie*
Manufacturing and prepress buyer: *Sherry Lewis*
Copy editor: *Laura A. Lawrie*
Editorial assistant: *Sasha Anderson*
Image permission coordinator: *Charles Morris*
Cover design: *Kiwi Design*

This book was set in 11/13 Plantin by DM Cradle Associates
and was printed and bound by Courier Companies, Inc.
The cover was printed by Phoenix Color Corp.

© 2003 by Pearson Education, Inc.
Upper Saddle River, New Jersey 07458

Printed in the United States of America

10   9   8   7   6   5   4   3   2   1

ISBN 0-13-098359-4

PEARSON EDUCATION LTD., London
PEARSON EDUCATION PTY, LIMITED, Sydney
PEARSON EDUCATION SINGAPORE, PTE. LTD.
PEARSON EDUCACION NORTH ASIA LTD., Hong Kong
PRENTICE-HALL CANADA, LTD., Toronto
PEARSON EDUCACIÓN DE MEXICO, S.A. DE C.V.
PEARSON EDUCATION--Japan, Tokyo
PEARSON EDUCATION MALAYSIA PTE., LTD.
PEARSON EDUCATION, Upper Saddle River, New Jersey

CONTENTS

ACKNOWLEDGMENTS

No book is a solo effort, and this brief manual is certainly no exception. I want to acknowledge the debt I owe my colleagues for their many wise suggestions and the many hours of discussion about student writing. I would like to single out one in particular, Dr. Priscilla Albright, whose wisdom and support over the past twenty years has been very much appreciated. I have enjoyed the long evening conversations over tea and coffee during countless College Art Association meetings.

I also wish to thank the staff at Prentice Hall for their patience. Wendy Yurash and Bud Therien have been generous with their time. Thanks are due as well to Laura Lawrie who guided the manuscript through its final stages. To the readers who gave their time and wisdom—Scott Karakas (University of North Carolina, Greensboro), Betty Brown (California State University, Northridge), Anthony Gully (Arizona State University), Laurina Dixon (Syracuse University), and Michael Hoff (University of Nebraska)— thank you as well. Finally, I wish to acknowledge my students in art history and American Studies and my husband's students in the School of Music and Dance at San José State University who tested sections of this text and provided valuable feedback.

This manual could not have been completed without the support and suggestions of my sons Matthew and Mitchell, my daughter-in-law Jimmée Greco, and my husband Daniel. Thank you all for tolerating my endless barrage of questions about the technical aspects of digital media and Internet access. I could not have completed Chapter 6 without your wise counsel. A special thank you as well to my husband who took time from his own teaching schedule to read and correct the many drafts as they evolved.

FIGURES

Figure 1 Sanchi, Madhya Pradesh, Raisen District
Stupa I
Eastern Gateway, view from east, detail:
    capital and yakshi
Circa first century B.C.
Buff Sandstone
Photo credit: American Institute of Indian
    Studies (AIIS) Neg. No.238.87

Figure 2 Ray Boynton,
California Agriculture
1937 (U.S. Treasury Section of Painting
    and Sculpture)
Modesto, California Post Office
Tempera on Mounted Plywood

Figure 3 *Kopereipi Emu*
Alligator River, Northern Territory,
Western Arnhem Land Australia
Pigment on Bark
Victoria Museum, Melbourne Australia
Reproduced courtesy of Museum Victoria

Figure 4   Gilbert Stuart, American, 1755–1828
Athenaeum Washington Original
Painting, 1796
Oil on Canvas
121.9 cm × 94 cm (48″ × 37″), Accurate.
William Francis Warden Fund, John H. and
   Ernestine A. Payne Fund, Commonwealth
   Cultural Preservation Trust
National Portrait Gallery, Smithsonian
   Institution; owned jointly with Museum of
   Fine Arts, Boston
Courtesy Museum of Fine Arts, Boston
Reproduced with permission
© 2002 Museum of Fine Arts, Boston
All Rights Reserved. Accession #: NPG.80.115

Figure 5   Hiram Powers,
Greek Slave
1847
Marble
Height 5′5 1/2″ (1.68m)
The Collection of the Newark Museum of
   Art
Gift of Franklin Murphy, Jr., 1926

Figure 6   Piet Mondrian, Dutch, 1872–1944
Composition with Red, Yellow, and Blue
Oil on Canvas,
1927
51.1 × 51.1cm (20 1/8 × 20 1/8″)
© Contemporary Collection of the Cleveland
   Museum of Art 1967.215
© Mondrian Holtzman Trust

Figure 7   Mu Qi (Mu Chi),
Six Persimmons
Southern Song (First half thirteenth century),
   China
Ink on Paper
Height 17 3/4″ (45.09cm)
Collection Ryokoin, Daitoku-ji, Kyoto

IMAGES ON THE INTERNET

In addition to the figures listed on pages ix to xi, other images discussed in *Looking and Writing* can be found on the Internet. They are listed below in order of their first appearance in the text. Many of these images also can be found on the companion websites of art history textbooks.

xvi: Cathedral of Notre Dame at Chartres: http://www.great-buildings.com/buildings/Chartres_Cathedral.html

3: Arthur Rothstein: http://memory.loc.gov/ammem/fsahtml/fachap05.html

23: Praxiteles, *Medici Venus:* http://harpy.uccs.edu/greek/sculpt/medici.jpg

32: Pablo Picasso, *Guernica*: http://grnica.swinternet.co.uk

33: Ndebele (Transvaal, South Africa): http://www.ux1.eiu.edu/~cfrb/paintedhouses.htm

39: William Harnett: *After the Hunt* (1885): http://search.famsf.org/4d.acgi$Search?list&=1&=william&=And&=Yes&=harnett&=&=&=Yes&=Yes&=f

39: August Rodin: http://www.rodinmuseum.org

40: Romare Bearden: http://www.beardenfoundation.org/

47: Jeff Koons: *Rabbit* (1986) http://broadartfoundation.org/collection/koons.html

49: *Venus of Willendorf:* http://vienna.cc/english/nhmuseum2.htm

INTRODUCTION

"Seeing is believing." "Look out below!" "I see what you mean." "Look on the bright side." When you entered kindergarten (if not before), you entered a world in which reading and writing skills took precedence over visual literacy. As you progressed through elementary and secondary school, your ability to read complex literature and your ability to write insightful (and grammatically correct) essays were indicators of your growing maturity. But people are actually very visual, as the above idioms remind us, and our ability to communicate visually is as important as our ability to communicate through the written word. When you opened your art history textbook for the first time, you may have noticed that the number of pictures reproduced far exceeds the number of illustrations in your history, literature, or science textbook. Unlike illustrations in other texts, the pictures in your art history textbook are not there to supplement or enliven the spoken and written text; the visual and written texts in art history books are partners in presenting information about the history of visual culture and visual literacy.

Keep in mind that the goal of universal literacy is a recent phenomenon in western history. For a much longer historical period, literacy was limited and the vast majority of people depended on the spoken word combined with visual imagery for information. Stained glass windows in French Gothic cathedrals (ca. twelfth–fourteenth centuries) such as those in the Cathedral of Notre Dame in Chartres (http://www.greatbuildings.com/ buildings/Chartres_Cathedral.html) functioned as an illustrated Bible, providing stories for the congregation to read as they attended mass (usually delivered in Latin, which the average churchgoer did not understand). Sculpture programs around the cathedral's doorways continued the sacred narratives, with images of Christ, Mary, the apostles, and prophets. Intertwined with biblical subjects were pre-Christian symbols such as the zodiac.

The experiences of Buddhist pilgrims at the temple and burial complex for the Buddha's ashes at Sanchi in central India are similar to those of French parishioners at Chartres. Built and expanded over three centuries (from the third century B.C.E. to the first century C.E.) the four *toranas* (gateways) that mark the cardinal directions around the largest burial mound (Stupa I) relate the stories *(jatakas)* of the Buddha's mortal life. Because early Buddhist art was *an-iconic* (without an image), artists adapted pre-Buddhist cosmic symbols (for example, the wheel, the lotus, the bull, and the elephant) to represent Buddhist concepts. A wheel, representing leadership as the Buddha "turns the wheel of law," dominates the narrative of the enlightenment of Sakyamuni (also called Siddhartha Gautama) under the bodhi tree, while the bull, representing the cosmic sign of his birth, is prominent in the birth panel. Another pre-Buddhist image adopted by Buddhist artists at Sanchi include the *yakshis*, female tree and fertility figures whose ancestry can be traced back to mother earth goddesses of the Indus Valley and the roots of Indian culture almost two thousand years earlier. A *yakshi* on the eastern *torana* of Stupa I (Fig. 1) languidly holds the branches of a mango tree, forming a graceful caryatid bracket between the vertical post and the first horizontal beam. The *yakshi* also may symbolize the birth of Gautama, the mortal Buddha. According to legend, Shakyamuni's mother Queen Maya was walking in her garden one day when she felt a twinge in her side. She seized a tree branch, which suddenly and miraculously flowered, and instantly gave birth to Gautama.

Some cultures did not develop an abstract written language in which symbols or marks represent sounds and therefore words, but relied on complex orality (the spoken word) with visual imagery. The Asante of Ghana communicated complex ideas on history, genealogy, religion, and moral and ethical responsibility through visual culture, as in the interplay of patterns and colors in the elaborate strip-woven *kente* cloth of the royal family and other dignitaries (http://users.erols.com/kemet/kente.htm). Over

Figure 1 The Eastern Gateway (*Torana*) of Stupa I at Sanchi combines Buddhist stories (*jatakas*) on the gently curved crossbeams with pre-Buddhist imagery in the *yakshi* that reaches for the fruiting branches of the mango.

three hundred geometric, color-rich patterns have been identified. Each functions as a mnemonic device to recall significant social, political, and cultural events in Asante history. Modern reproductions of *kente* cloth have become significant symbols of black pride in African-American communities and can be found on diverse objects including graduation collars, Kwanzaa (December 25–January 1) holiday cloth, and calendars.

These examples remind us that we are surrounded by visual information in our daily lives. When we participate in a conversation or attend a lecture, we are attentive to more than the words we hear with their tonal qualities; we look for visual clues. We observe body language, facial expression, and gesture to help us interpret what is said. Presentation and body language, together with sound cues, tell us if the speaker is happy or sad, jesting or serious, calm or angry, trustworthy or unreliable. Like the Asante, we examine what the speaker is wearing and the colors and patterns in the cloth to ascertain the credibility of the speaker. These daily analytic experiences are carried with us when we attend a concert, listen to a compact disc, or look at paintings, sculpture, drawings, photographs, and other visual materials. Taught these skills as children, they are part of our enculturation, the learned behavior that identifies us as a member of a specific dynamic culture. This is why as outsiders (for example, when we travel) we may misinterpret visual clues; with increased exposure, we become acculturated to a different, equally valid, set of interpretations.

With so many possibilities for misinterpretation, we might ask ourselves how we know how to see if seeing is a cultural practice and not a physiological phenomenon. The notion that psychology rather than physiology determined how people perceive the world fascinated late nineteenth-century philosophers, theoreticians, writers, and artists; the resulting debates and scientific research are crucial to an understanding of early modern art. Marita Sturken and Lisa Cartwright, in *Practices of Looking* (Oxford University Press, 2001), and Nicholas Mirzoeff, in *An Introduction to Visual Culture* (Routledge, 1999), emphasize the extraordinary power of visual imagery to shape and not simply reflect our perceptions of the world. In response to images, we subconsciously scan a checklist of likely meanings, evaluate them, and arrive at the most logical interpretation—all accomplished within a split second. This is especially true with computer-generated video and other media that exist in time. A viewer may only have a glimpse of an image when it is displayed on a monitor, unlike paintings, sculpture, and print media, in which an image remains stable over time. During that split second, the viewer must both register the image and determine its meaning.

This brief manual is a guide to help develop strategies for improving your visual literacy skills. Representational images are perceived on many levels, from their denotative (descriptive) meanings to their connotative (implied) meanings and are best understood through the interweaving of historical, sociopolitical, biographical, symbolic/mythological, and formalist analysis. They serve as both positive and negative bellwethers of prevailing ideas and values of a specific time and place. For example, consider the post office murals funded by United States Treasury Department during the Great Depression. These projects provided positive images of American workers and an interpretation of American history designed to bolster the battered spirits of American citizens. President Franklin D. Roosevelt, in fact, emphasized his desire that artists present positive American images in an American style to an American public. A mural in the Modesto, California, Post Office (Fig. 2), painted by Ray Boynton, introduces a successful farmer and his wife with their crops spread out before them like a cornucopia. A post office patron immediately sees this descriptive or denotative meaning. To fully understand this post office mural, however, one must learn something about the depressed agricultural economy in the 1930s, not only in the Dust Bowl states but also in California. The Modesto mural presents the ideal farm and farmer, a paean to pre-Depression stability and post-Depression success, not an image of present conditions. A professor in American Studies may choose to interpret this mural symbolically, drawing on Thomas Jefferson's assertion of the yeoman (independent) farmer as the backbone of the United States. A sociopolitical analyst may discuss the gendered roles of the farmer and the farmer's wife while an economist discusses the marketplace and its impact on the successful planter. A researcher in Ethnic Studies would focus on the absence in the mural of the Mexican *braceros* and Mexican American farm workers who labored in the fields.

An artist's history is equally important. What experiences, prejudices, and talents does the artist bring to a work? Artists selected for post office commissions often were not chosen from the pool of local artists with personal connections to the region but by juried national competitions. An urban artist may have a very different perception of an agricultural community than an artist raised on a farm.

Figure 2 *California Agriculture* (1937), one of twelve lunettes painted by Ray Boynton in the Modesto (California) Post Office, was commissioned by the federal government during the Great Depression to provide positive images of American life.

An Eastern artist may not know the agricultural labor history of California. In the Modesto example, the artist Ray Boynton taught a course in mural painting at the California School of Fine Arts in San Francisco; his assistants were drawn from the regional Works Progress Administration pool of local artists.

The discussion above of the implied or connotative meanings of the mural relied on a structural analysis, a form of contemporary analysis that draws from literary reading skills to uncover meaning. Some art historians also explore an artist's working practices in a formal analysis. A formal analysis questions and examines the very tools used by an artist. How has the artist handled color, line, space, shape, perspective, and light? What design principles were chosen to create a sense of visual harmony, balance, and focus? Since the mural mentioned above is one in a series of thirteen paintings completed for the post office, you would have to ask how the artist integrated this lunette (moon-shaped) into the other mural panels. Is this integrated as a continuous narrative (story) that has a beginning, middle, and end, or did Boynton organize and integrate the panels by repeating specific elements of form and design to lead the spectator's eyes from one panel to the next wherever we begin to look at the sequence? A thorough interpretation of this mural will combine as many of these approaches as possible to establish meaning.

Looking and Writing is divided into eight chapters that expand the ideas presented in this introduction. Skill tests at the conclusion of Chapters One through Six help you apply the material as it is presented.

Chapter 1, "Looking and Seeing," introduces the ways in which we examine imagery and assign meaning to signs and symbols. Chapter 2, "Looking for Meaning," presents different interpretive methodologies. We ask whether meaning is inherent in a work or is brought to the work by the viewer. We have already touched on this idea above in the discussion of the Modesto Post Office mural. Would an art historian, an economic historian, or an ethnic historian emphasize different salient features in a discussion of the mural? How would a local Modesto resident using the post office understand our example? Have the resident's and the historians' interpretations changed as we move further from the actual experiences of the Great Depression? The next two chapters outline basic tenets of formal analysis (Chapter 3) and principles of design and composition (Chapter 4). These four chapters together present some of the basic concerns in the analysis of artwork and other forms of visual communication (descriptive subject, interpretive content, and formal construction).

"Applying Art History's Tools" in Chapter 5 takes students out of the classroom and into a museum, gallery, or other exhibition or public art space. Many students in introductory classes have had limited museum experiences; this chapter suggests ways in which a museum or gallery visit can be organized to maximize time and minimize confusion. Chapter 5 starts with basic information, suggesting what to bring to an exhibit and how to organize notes to collect accurate and sufficient information for your assignment. Using the Internet to visit a virtual museum or to research online images is introduced in Chapter 6.

Once a student has gathered information, the next task is to organize it coherently into an essay. Chapter 7, "Writing Your Essay," suggests some guidelines in organizing research, finding a topic or a subject on which to write, exploring methodologies for writing, and selecting an appropriate vocabulary. Included at the end of Chapter 7 is a list of common vocabulary mistakes to aid a student during proofreading. The uses and forms of citation suggested by the Modern Language Association (MLA) and the *Chicago Manual of Style* are presented in Chapter 8.

A list of readings on the subjects of writing and analysis, critical thinking, and symbolic meaning is included at the end of the text.

I
LOOKING AND SEEING

Leonardo da Vinci believed that sight was one of the most important, if not *the* most important, of our five senses, because we understand the world through our eyes. Three centuries later, the American transcendental philosopher Ralph Waldo Emerson likened himself to a transparent eyeball absorbing the sensations of the natural world. Both Leonardo and Emerson distinguished between the physical process of seeing and the intellectual process of knowing, that is, between the ability to see and the ability to look. Whereas we tend to use the terms interchangeably in everyday speech, they are distinctly different, similar to the distinction between sight and insight. Although we often use the word *see* to indicate understanding, even perception beyond what is immediately seen, as in the case of a soothsayer or Seer, *to see* is a physiological trait; light hits our retinas and images are transferred to the brain. The brain unscrambles the signals it receives and sends back a translation. In everyday speech, we use the word *look* to mean *glance*, but to look is a cognitive process that requires interpretation. In *The Intelligent Eye* (The Getty Trust, 1994), David Perkins distinguishes between the "perceptual eye" that, like a camera, records a scene without interpretation, and the "hungry (or intelligent) eye" that looks beyond and beneath appearances through the application of deliberate reasoning. In this way, the eye looks not for what is immediately visible, but what is invisible. If we look again at the post office mural discussed in the introduction (Fig. 2), we readily see the farmer and his wife with their abundance of vegetables and other farm produce; this is the visible world that our eye records. The suggested meanings we bring to our discussion of the tableau form the invisible world.

We are taught to decipher images, moving from the visible to the invisible, in much the same way we are taught to read words. Parents teach children to interpret pictures. Mastery of this skill enables children to differentiate one shape from another and to properly identify them. Learned perception rather than innate perception helps us differentiate between a real object and the abstraction of that object in another medium. They learn that the picture of a horn represents the object "horn." Some learn to attach the sound of a horn to its picture.

Children who have learned to connect the real object and its abstraction in picture books learn to read more quickly than those who have not acquired this skill. In the novel *Foe*, the South African writer J. M. Coetzee creates the character Friday, an isolated man from a desolate island, and transports him to London. Having lived his developmental life removed from any trappings of Western culture, Friday responds like an infant and must be taught cultural survival skills. During the process of acculturation, he is shown photographs of himself, yet he cannot identify them. He sees himself in a mirror, yet he cannot recognize himself. Why? Coetzee suggests that Friday had no experience with abstracted visual representations and therefore did not have the necessary tools with which to interpret them. To Friday, the photographs and the mirror were arrangements of shapes, lines, and colors that he could not organize. The reflected and photographed images were removed from the real world in which he lived. Without training, Friday did not have the ability to see the real world in the abstracted image. While we know that the worlds of television and film are not real, the images that move across the screen make sense to us because, unlike Friday, we have learned the appropriate interpretive tools that permit these arrangements of lines, colors, and shapes to communicate.

Photography, in fact, presents an interesting dilemma for visual analysis, the fine line between truth and fiction. Many people see photographs as inherently truthful documents. Perhaps you have heard the phrase "A camera cannot lie." Yet, photographs are as much about the eye and intent of the photographer as they are about perceptions of reality. A photographer can modify the angle of vision (shooting from below or above the subject), alter the focus (from crisp or sharp to soft or blurred), change the depth of field (to compress or expand the depth based on clarity or focus), and control the exposure (the length of time film or digital media is exposed) when shooting. In both the darkroom and the computer graphics application, contrast, color (including both local and arbitrary color), and focus can be altered.

Arthur Rothstein (http://memory.loc.gov/ammem/fsahtml/fachap05.html), a photographer with the Farm Security Administration (FSA) in the Roosevelt era shot one of the most famous photographs of the Depression, a boy and his father braving a dust cloud. Unlike the images of fecund farms commissioned for post offices (Fig. 2), the FSA employed photographers to document the dusted-out and tractored-out farms. They wanted to chronicle the parched, wind-blown farms and the urban breadlines. Among Rothstein's photographs is an isolated bovine skull resting on the dry, sandy soil of a once-fertile farm in the Dakotas. It was a poignant image, widely published, of the death of agricultural prosperity. Later it was reported that Rothstein had moved the skull a few feet to increase the impact of the shot. Republicans opposed to Roosevelt's New Deal politics condemned the photograph. They called the skull a propaganda ploy used to magnify the impact of Dust Bowl conditions in the Dakotas and gain sympathy for Democratic environmental legislation. Does the staging of a photograph or event make it dishonest? When Rothstein moved the skull to create a more poignant image, did he invalidate the losses suffered by farmers in Oklahoma, Arkansas, and the Dakotas?

As suggested in the introduction, seeing is culturally based. That is, how we see determines what we see. An Aboriginal Northern Australian painter from the Alligator River region of Western Arnhem Land presents an Emu (Fig. 3) by simultaneously describing the skeletal structure, the internal organs, and the external outline in a style known as X-ray or in-fill painting. The Australian artist's work captures the essence of the animal, not its outward appearance. The painting reflects the power of creation and the spiritual world within an animistic belief system in which the spark of creation, called Dreamtime (*Jukurrpa*) by Australian Aboriginals, remains embedded in the features of the land and all who inhabit it. The painting of the Emu provides a tangible image of an event within creation and becomes an active participant in the ritual and ceremonial life of the community. The Emu in this painting exists on the threshold between

Figure 3 The visible skeleton of this Aboriginal Australian X-ray or in-fill Emu refers to Dreamtime or the time of creation. Emu is a powerful Dreaming Spirit associated with men, the fire ceremony (Tjarri Warnpa), and maintaining and protecting the law (tradition).

the world of people and the world of the ancestors in Dreamtime, so its image is both of this world (the external outline) and beyond this world (the internal organs). For this reason, its visible (earthly) and invisible (spiritual) essences are shown. In contrast, a Western-trained artist might describe an Emu through a detailed visual description of its external characteristics, concentrating on color, proportions, and surface textures, and the Emu's spatial location, but not the internal, unseen skeleton and viscera.

COMMUNICATING WITH SIGNS AND SYMBOLS

Communication is crucial to a group's success. Human cultures rely on their shared symbolic languages to communicate and perpetuate secular and sacred traditions. Shared meanings define and differentiate societies, creating in the process outsiders, those unfamiliar with the symbolic or metaphoric language of the group, and insiders, for whom specific images or symbols carry considerable weight.

Artists manipulate the visual language of their group and thus provide meaningful communication. We can construct two systems of visual literacy from which to draw. One is a system of graphic signs. Unlike contemporary literary signs, graphic signs provide information but do not carry meaning beyond their immediate presence or use. When we study for a driver's license, we memorize the graphic signs that provide road instructions—stop, yield, merge, and so on. We may notice that a sign's shape is determined by the information it conveys; for example, square red and white signs provide regulatory information, while yellow diamond shaped signs warn drivers of specific road hazards. With frequent exposure, the color and shape alone will carry meaning.

A second system of images is symbolic. Symbolic meanings may be ascribed to people (for an American, the meaning(s) of George Washington), places (for the Japanese, the meaning(s) of Mt. Fuji), or objects (for the Navajo, the meaning(s) in the shape and patterns of a woven basket). Because these images carry meaning both on the surface and below the surface, symbolic languages are the most intriguing yet also the most difficult to understand. Unlike signs, symbols are culturally specific, so an "outsider," as discussed above, may never fully comprehend the deepest meaning of a particular symbol. Symbols, unlike signs, also are dynamic, changing over time to meet shifting cultural needs. Therefore, the accrued meanings of a symbol are more elusive.

Every visual text must be interpreted. But how do we determine meaning from the signs and symbols if they are not stable? If each viewer brings unique personal experiences to an image, is there a right and wrong response? Does the image always say the same thing? Will it say the same thing to all people who see it? Again, we touched on this idea in the introduction when discussing the Modesto Post Office mural (Fig. 2) and its multiple possible interpretations.

Questions of meaning have always intrigued us. Jacques Derrida, a contemporary French philosopher interested in the meaning of signs (such as words) within language (a study called semiology), posed the following question in his book *The Truth in Painting*. What did the French post-Impressionist painter Paul Cézanne mean in his brief letter to a friend when he said, "Let me tell you the truth about painting"? Is there some great philosophic or spiritual truth that Cézanne wished to examine? Did Cézanne want to discuss the importance of gesture and the body language of the process? Maybe there was an anecdote that Cézanne wished to share. As Derrida suggests, Cézanne's statement is ambiguous despite its apparent simplicity. The question that Derrida asks, however, is one we shall examine further. When we see an object or image, how do we begin to unravel its meaning(s)? What questions must we ask ourselves?

Think about the portrait in Figure 4. You probably recognize it as George Washington, although you might not know that the artist is Gilbert Stuart or that it was painted in 1796. This image by Stuart is an archetypal image; it is the model for many later representations of President Washington. How many different meanings can be assigned to this portrait? A list of adjectives might include honesty, integrity, powerful, perseverant, independent. Other lists might focus on anecdotes and stories about Washington (the cherry tree, the hardships at Valley Forge, his wooden teeth), on his many occupations (soldier, surveyor, planter, statesman, president), or on his maxims ("I cannot tell a lie", "first in the hearts of his countrymen", "father of the country"). Not all associations to Washington were or are positive; in the eighteenth century, King George III and the parliament of Great Britain called him a rebel, a traitor, and a radical, while some contemporary historians discuss his role as a slave owner and land speculator. All of these meanings are attached, consciously or unconsciously, to the Washington portrait whether we see his likeness reproduced by the federal government on the dollar bill, by an advertising firm selling cherry pies for Presidents' Day, or elsewhere.

Figure 4 This Gilbert Stuart portrait of George Washington (1796) is the archetype for many subsequent images of the first president of the United States. Stuart's image blends two views of Washington: Washington, the man and Washington, the president. Courtesy, Museum of Fine Arts, Boston. Reproduced with permission. © 2002 Museum of Fine Arts, Boston. All rights reserved.

TESTING YOUR SKILLS: LOOKING AND SEEING

Developing visual literacy skills takes practice. Choose a mundane or ordinary object to describe and write down your immediate observations without sorting or analyzing them. Continue to record what you see until you feel that you have exhausted every possible aspect of the object. Your list probably includes both observable data (size, color, texture, shape, light and shadow, for example) and associative data (references to experiences with that or a similar object).

You may want to compare your responses to those of a friend or classmate studying the same object. Are the lists similar? Where and how do they differ? You would expect associative references to be different because you and your friend or classmate have different life experiences. But, are the observable data (line, color, texture, and space, for example) the same? Careful observation is essential to the study of visual media, but how visual information is processed is individual.

The next step in developing visual literacy is to take the information gathered through careful and deliberate observation and to assess its meaning.

2
LOOKING FOR MEANING

SUBJECT MATTER AND CONTENT

As we discovered when looking at the Gilbert Stuart portrait of George Washington, meaning is not constant but fluid, not singular but multiple. Meaning is modified by individual experiences and by cultural expectations and norms. Paintings and sculpture of female nudes, common in the work of nineteenth-century artists such as that of the American sculptor Hiram Powers's *Greek Slave* (1843) (Fig. 5) were approached differently in the late twentieth-century because of an increased sensitivity to issues of gender, race, and class. This leads us to one of the first points that we must consider when we look at a work of art—the difference between *subject matter* and *meaning or content*. The subject matter of the work in Figure 5 is a female in chains, and in Figure 4 the portrait of an elderly man. But their meanings are much more complex.

When Hiram Powers carved *Greek Slave*, the nineteenth-century economic and social environments of the United States and Europe were in flux as a result of increased industrialization, territorial expansion, growing nationalism, and, in the United States, increased friction between the North and the South. The political and social turmoil coupled with population displacement, deteriorating urban centers, and a growing concern for the decline of personal rights fostered a

Figure 5 *Greek Slave* by Hiram Powers (1847) was seen by more than one hundred thousand people when it toured the United States in 1848. According to its promotional literature, the image represented uncompromising virtue in the face of degradation, inward purity, and the force of character.

sense of alienation and hopelessness, what historians have called "the modern condition." This, in turn led to the defining characteristics of the European and American Romantic periods—exoticism, eroticism, and escapism. Writers and artists imagined past cultures as purer and less polluted than their own. One such historical period was ancient Greece.

Ancient Greece held a special fascination for Europeans and Americans as the foundation (together with Rome and ancient Egypt) of Western culture. Therefore, the Greek war of independence waged against the Ottoman Empire of Turkey in the 1830s was of particular concern, because it disrupted the symbolic foundation of Western culture. The struggle pitted two centuries-old rivals: Christian Europeans and Middle Eastern Muslims. The *Times* of London and the American Horace Greeley's abolitionist *Liberator* fueled the emotional response of what politicians in Great Britain dubbed "the Eastern Question" by sensationalizing the presumed sale of white women into slavery by Turkish merchants. Powers's *Greek Slave* (Fig. 5) is a Christian Greek woman (look for the clue on the pillar that provides this part of her identity) in chains who was captured by the Turks to be sold at a slave auction. Enchained, stripped of clothing, and exposed to the libidinous stares of prospective buyers, Powers condemns Turkey as her ruthless and barbaric captor while appealing to Western European considerations of morality and virtue. This becomes part of the meaning of the sculpture. Powers further reinforces cultural memory by casting his subject as a Hellenistic (ca. third–second centuries B.C.E.) image of Venus familiar to educated audiences in both the United States and Europe.

Description and Analysis

A thoughtful discussion of a work of art must distinguish not only between subject matter and content but also between description and analysis. A reader experiences an object through a combination of objective description and subjective interpretation. A description provides observed details while an analysis probes behind those details for meaning. A description of Figure 4 might begin, "In this unfinished portrait, an elderly man is presented in a three-quarter view. The subject's head is placed in the upper third of the canvas with his chin resting almost at the midpoint. Light falls evenly across his face, emphasizing his features and creating shadows across his temples and the sides of his face. His white hair, suggested by many short brushstrokes, curls at his cheekbones. His eyebrow line curves to meet the bridge of his prominent nose, suggesting the upper outline of a heart. His eyes are deep set and focus on the viewer." To continue this discussion, the writer might comment on the colors (especially his excessively rosy cheeks), the ambiguous figure-ground relationship (where the sitter is in reference to the space), and the repetition of lines (the diagonals of the hair line and the jacket lapels). What do we learn about the sitter from this portrait? What must be added to turn this description into an analysis?

By adding just a few adjectives and including subjective value judgments to the description, we transform a description into an analysis. For example, if we add the following sentence to the description above, we move beyond description to suggest something about the character of the sitter: "There is a sense of assured power and dignity in this portrait, created by the uncompromising gaze of his deep-set eyes, his pursed lips, and the tense line of his jaw." He does not simply look at the viewer but stares resolutely, uncompromisingly outward. The suggestion that there is tension not only in his jaw but also in his closed mouth contributes information about the sitter's character as well.

Although the portrait was left unfinished, Gilbert Stuart painted a timeless, unpretentious yet ennobled study of the first president of the United States that, despite its lack of adornment or other symbols of official status, is among the nation's most powerful symbols.

Interpretive Methodologies

Of course, it would be simple if the search for meaning ended here, but it doesn't, as you discovered in the discussion of Washington's portrait. Distinguishing between subject and content is only the first step in understanding a visual image. Analytic systems drawn from a century of social science theory as well as discussions of formal properties are used to understand content and to move from mere description to analysis. French theorists such as Roland Barthes and Jacques Derrida suggest that no work contains only a single meaning; meaning exists on multiple levels, some clearly presented on the surface, some veiled or implied, and some hidden deep within cultural memory. Their methodology for analyzing these layers of meaning is derived from a century of structural theory introduced first by the Swiss linguist Ferdinand de Saussure.

Structuralism and Post-Structuralism

Ferdinand de Saussure suggested that language is the product of cultural conventions and is not imbedded in the actual sounds of the words we use. We accept that the four letters "e," "r," "t," and "e," when placed in a specific order, "t","," "r," "e," "e," forms a word in English that is recognized as "tree." The word tree (which Saussure calls a signifier) creates the mental image of a tree (that which is signified) when we read or hear it; together, the signifier and what is signified form a linguistic sign. It is through a culturally accepted arrangement of linguistic signs that we communicate. There are now three questions for us to consider. What tree do you see? Does your neighbor see the same tree that you do? Why does the combination of these four letters produce a tree in your imagination and not a book? After all, both have four letters, two consonants, and two identical vowels. The third question on this list addresses the idea of language as a series of arbitrary cultural conventions. The first two questions address the fluidity of meaning. By the way, if we were French-speaking, this combination of these four letters would not stimulate us to visualize a tree at all. In their proper French order, these letters form the infinitive of the verb "to be," "être."

Under Saussure's model, language is a collective cultural construction that permits people to communicate. Even within language, there is variety, what we popularly call dialects, and what linguists call individual speech performance (as opposed to cultural language structure). An American can distinguish without too much difficulty between a New Yorker and a Texan. They each speak American English, but a New Yorker's daily speech may be sprinkled with Yiddish words, while there are more words that are Spanish in a Texan's daily speech.

The French anthropologist Claude Levi-Strauss applied Saussure's linguistic theory to the study of culture. Levi-Strauss examined cultural systems (language) and cultural practice (speech) to determine why cultures developed as they did. He established a basis for interpreting mythmaking in society, the stories each society creates about its origins and values. According to Levi-Strauss, cultures create myths to address and resolve contradictions and to maintain a sense of order or balance. His research suggested that stories or myths exist on multiple levels, from the surface narrative understood by young children and the uninitiated to more complex metaphoric and allegoric references understood by the elders and the initiated. This hierarchy of meaning is similar to our earlier discussion about subject matter and content or between description and analysis.

Roland Barthes, mentioned earlier in this chapter, used Saussure's and Levi-Strauss's structural models for his analysis, but he believed that neither Saussure nor Levi-Strauss pursued their analyses far enough. He suggested that the meanings they discovered after the first stage of analysis could lead to another, deeper, analysis. According to Barthes, every idea we uncover through analysis can be used as the starting point for a new line of questions. Meaning is not stable but an ever-changing product of interpretation. We can apply Barthes's *poststructural* methodology to understanding the tree mentioned earlier. We look at the picture of a brown vertical support with a green canopy of leaves and determine that it is a "tree." This is only the first step, because "tree" is rather general. Barthes calls this "primary signification." If we look more closely at the image, we discover that there are round red balls hanging among the green leaves. We can now move from the general "tree" to a more specific tree, an "apple tree." To simplify this discussion, I am leaving out an analytic step that defines the red globes among the leaves as apples and not cherries, red plums, or Christmas ornaments. "Apple tree" becomes a second, more precise level of meaning or signification. Shall we stop here? Not necessarily, because Western Christian culture has attached specific meanings to the apple tree and its fruit. An apple tree can be a complex metaphor for the Garden of Eden, Adam and Eve, and the Fall of Humankind.

To understand the next step in the analysis, we must look at the context of the apple tree. Where is it? In an orchard? With a man, a woman, and a serpent? In a backyard with a large tire swing? The peripheral information or context will shape the outcome of our analysis. The process of studying signs within language systems to uncover meaning is called semiology. The methodology of semiology has been applied by some art historians to understand how images work within cultures.

Through our analysis of the apple tree, we were able to *deconstruct* it, examine it in detail and discover some of its denotative and connotative (implied) meanings. Like Roland Barthes, Jacques Derrida suggests that these meanings are not constant but change with time, mood, place, and other contextual variables. For the poststructuralist Derrida, every linguistic sign contains within itself multiple meanings; some are "present" (overt or near the surface) while others may be "deferred" (covert or below the surface). We understand a sign (word or image) because of its context (the text or other signs around it). The series of questions above that asked you to consider the location of the apple tree (an orchard, a religious text, a botany textbook, or a gardening manual) helps to establish the context of the tree. But the apple tree may also evoke memories of previous experiences or memories that color the way you look it. Derrida calls this information "traces." Go back to the exercise at the end of Chapter 1. The nonobservable references on your list are the "traces" of meaning suggested by Derrida.

When we look at a painting, drawing, sculpture, or photograph, we examine the visual signs for meaning. These signs are in the subject matter as well as the arrangement of colors, spaces, lines, and forms.

Structuralism and post-Structuralism are methodologies or systems used to organize an analysis. Other interpretive strategies, also drawn from the social sciences, include Gender Studies (Feminism and Gay/Lesbian Studies), Orientalism (including Colonial and Postcolonial Studies), and Historical Context (Marxist). These methodologies employ the process of structural analysis, that is, looking at and below the surface for meaning; however, each asks a different set of questions.

Feminist criticism and Gay/Lesbian Studies question gender and sexuality in relation to social attitudes and expectations. Furthermore, as gender studies, they investigate whether the roles individuals play in society are cultural (learned) or natural (biological). Are males considered rational and females irrational because culture makes them so, or is there a biological determinant? Gender studies also include an evaluation of the gender or sexual orientation of the artist as it relates to a completed work. Both Feminist and Gay/Lesbian criticism rely heavily on social theories about the construction of individual identity within society.

Orientalism and the related fields of colonial and postcolonial studies, examine the uneven distribution of power based on race and ethnicity. The premises of Orientalism are not new; they have been part of the West's attitudes toward the East for centuries. However, the identification and discussion of the bias of colonial superiority in Western thought and its impact on the arts was introduced in the 1978 book *Orientalism*, by Edward Said. Said proposed that the East has always held a special place in Western consciousness, helping to define Western material and intellectual culture by presenting its opposite or antithesis. He suggests that the premise of Western superiority and power is based on constructed assumptions of the East's inferiority and impotence.

Sometimes called "New Art History," art historians and critics interested in a Marxist analysis start from the perspective of social history to study political, class, and economic struggles and their impact on the arts. A Marxist analysis includes a consideration of historical events and their role in shaping an artist's perspective.

These analytic systems are models used to study a work of art within a specific culture. We can turn once again to Hiram Powers's *Greek Slave* (Fig. 5) to demonstrate their application.

Feminism

The enchained woman is fully revealed to the viewer; there are no draperies to cover her modesty. She faces resolutely downward across her left shoulder, thus avoiding a direct gaze and confrontation with either her captor or buyer (both metaphorically represented by the viewing audience). Her body language is not at all assertive. A Feminist reading of this work would emphasize her submissive nature and discuss the tractable role of women within a patriarchal system. The chains reinforce the reading of *Greek Slave* as a victimized woman, alluding to the relationship between bondage, power, and eroticism.

A popular Western social theory in the early and middle nineteenth-century, coinciding with Powers's carving of *Greek Slave*, placed women within a protective social environment that the anthropologist Nancy Cott characterized as the "cult of true womanhood." Women created the private islands of Christian and domestic calm within the turbulent seas of a public industrial world. Women's magazines during this period reinforced the domestic and nurturing responsibilities of women within the family. The idealized nude *Greek Slave* both reinforced, through associative anecdotes, and challenged concepts of nineteenth-century maidenly virtue. When Powers's *Greek Slave* was shown in England at the Crystal Palace World Exposition in 1851, it was carefully screened from women by a thick velvet curtain so that women's moral strength and assumed purity, two of the tenets of the cult of true womanhood, would not be compromised. Only on "woman's day" at the Fair, when no men were permitted, would the curtain be drawn so that a woman could look at this marble sculpture. This historical anecdote raises a number of questions. Is there a difference between the male gaze (the process of looking) and the female gaze? Does any implied difference rest with the subject matter or with social and cultural expectations of morality and virtue? Did the restricted viewing of *Greek Slave* add an element of male voyeurism to the work? Given the paternalism of the nineteenth-century, how would a nineteenth-century man have approached this sculpture? Does this information add to the original meaning of Hiram Powers's *Greek Slave*? Does it change or expand her meaning? You may also want to think about the difference between Powers's supple young vulnerable female nude and a similar image in *Playboy*. This question now goes to the intent of the producer and the assumptions of the audience, and carries the work forward to our current set of social interpretations.

Orientalism

Now, let us approach the work in question from an Orientalist perspective. In the nineteenth century, when issues of modesty and decorum isolated western women, exotic non-European women (mostly from the Middle East and North Africa) became popular subjects for artists, as did stories of Middle Eastern barbarism and depravity versus Western compassion and honor. Although Powers's innocent (and presumably pure) manacled captive is not a Middle Eastern woman, *Greek Slave* would appeal to late Romantic assumptions of exoticism and eroticism; at the same time, it affirms the belief in Eastern barbarism in contrast to Western humanitarianism. Notice that the last two categories (Feminist criticism and Orientalism) are not mutually exclusive.

An extended interpretation of Said's Orientalist methodology considers the way in which a dominant culture defines nonmembers. The premise of Orientalism, the uneven distribution of power based on race and ethnicity, has been applied in the United States to Native American, Latino/Chicano, and African American studies.

Related to Orientalism is *colonialism*, understood to imply an uneven relationship involving intellectual superiority and exploitation. Such an analysis traditionally investigated the economic and political impact on both the colonizer and the colonized (for example, Great Britain and the American colonies prior to 1776) and the resulting unequal distribution of power. Although once restricted to political systems, the methodologies of colonialist analysis now extend the consequences of dominance and submission beyond political systems to include any relationship in which power is unequal. Colonialist premises (assumptions of superiority versus inferiority and issues of paternalism and infantilism) also are present in discussions of Orientalism and Feminism. It is in this context, for example, that we can discuss *Greek Slave*. Who holds the more powerful position (that is, who is in control), the manacled woman or the viewer (who, by extension, may represent her captor, her buyer, or her liberator)?

Historical and Contextual Criticism (Marxist Criticism)

Finally, we can understand *Greek Slave* within the parameters of growing nationalism (in Europe) and the need to reinforce nationalist values in the United States. The confrontation between abolitionist ideology and proslavery forces in the United States threatened the solidarity and stability of the Union. American writers and artists in the early nineteenth century, including Powers, often used metaphors to present antislavery arguments, so their audience in the 1840s may well have assigned an abolitionist interpretation to *Greek Slave*. Because American democratic principles were based on Classical (Greek and Roman) models, the enslavement of Greece thus could be read as allusions both to slavery in the United States on the eve of the Civil War and to the bondage of American political values of freedom and egalitarianism.

While these analytic methodologies may seem very unfamiliar, they actually are not. As discussed earlier, we are surrounded by images from a variety of media in our daily lives. Advertising agencies and marketing firms rely on the power of images and our ability to read even very subtle messages presented visually. A commercial in 1999 by a parcel shipping firm played with ideas of feminism and masculinity when it presented toy soldiers in women's undergarments. Although the subject of the thirty-second television spot was the efficiency of one shipping firm compared to its competitors, it would not have worked successfully if the audience could not decipher the encoded meaning (that women's lingerie was inappropriate for combat soldiers in the field). Similarly, the Gilbert Stuart portrait of Washington appears in many advertisements, especially in February. These advertising agencies are asking you, as the viewer, to remember the many meanings attached to Washington and to apply them to the product they are promoting.

Drawn from a century of borrowed social science theory applied to the visual arts, the analytic methodologies discussed above add to the meaning of *Greek Slave*. Familiarity with the context of a work adds to our enjoyment and understanding. But these methodologies can only be understood as part of the interpretation of any single work of art. They are pathways in a continual process of discovery toward a work's many meanings.

Although some art historians desire to ascertain "the" meaning in a work of art, meaning changes over time as we learn more and bring new experiences to a work. Unlike mathematics in which the sum of two given numbers will always be the same, critical interpretation in the arts is fluid; there *is* no single "truth" when we discuss meaning. Perhaps that is what Cézanne meant in his very ambiguous comment discussed earlier. And, that is why great works of art have very long lives. Viewers enjoy looking again and again at the same painting, sculpture, print, photograph, or drawing, because there is always something new to discover when we take the time to look. Remember that we, as viewers, are important to the work of art that we are studying because we bring our own unique experiences, knowledge, and viewpoint to that work and disseminate those attitudes into our world.

Other Interpretive Considerations

Other approaches that an art historian may combine with historical or contextual analyses include *style*; *biography*; *technique*; *process and media*; and *iconography and iconology*.

Style

Style is twofold. First, it is the characteristic way in which an artist chooses to represent the world, a visual response to experiences and events. It also is the visual conventions of a particular place at a particular time. The style of an individual artist allows us to differentiate between the paintings of, for example, Michelangelo and Leonardo da Vinci. Just as each individual has a unique fingerprint, so, too, do artists have unique styles that include the preparation of a canvas before painting, draftsmanship, lighting preferences, and brushstroke. Michelangelo and Leonardo, however, are both Renaissance artists, so they also share the *visual conventions* of that historical period despite their personal stylistic differences.

Style is not static, either within the lifetime of an artist or within the historical life of a culture or society. It undergoes myriad cycles as it changes to meet new stimuli. An examination of the work of the twentieth-century artist Pablo Picasso reveals shifts in his style as he moved from the paintings of his youth, through the cubist and classicizing works of his early career, to the complex mixture of his personal styles in his mature work.

Two contrasting twentieth-century styles are *abstraction* and *realism*. Abstract art starts with an object or subject and, through a process of simplification and elimination, reduces that object or subject to its most essential representational form that continues to carry meaning. The cubist works of Picasso are examples of abstraction; there is always an object present, although it may not be immediately obvious to the viewer. For Picasso, the loss of the object meant the loss of meaning in painting. He personally could not work in the *nonobjective* (sometimes called nonrepresentational style that some of his contemporaries such as Piet Mondrian (Fig. 6) pursued.

Although nonobjective works are not derived from lived experiences or environments, they should not be regarded as meaningless decorations. In his book on new painting (*Painting and Pure Painting*), Mondrian suggested that pure or nonrepresentational painting carried the viewer away from the limitations of the mundane world into a higher plane of spiritual awareness.

Realists try faithfully to record the world around them, even if the actual subject matter cannot be experienced (for example, a painting of Adam and Eve in the Garden of Eden). Important to the work of realists is the paramount need for identifiable content. Ray Boynton's mural in the Modesto, California post office (Fig. 2) falls within the tradition of realism.

A close relative of realism is *naturalism*; what distinguishes realism from naturalism is the importance placed on meaning. Naturalism is an artistic device borrowed from literary theory in which artists appear to record without comment the world around them. Naturalism is considered a more objective representation while realism is subjective interpretation.

A subdivision of naturalism is *conceptual realism,* representing not what you see but what you know you *should* see, as if your eye were similar to the nondiscriminatory lens of a camera. The storefront paintings by the mid-twentieth-century artist Richard Estes demonstrate this. Unlike the objective camera eye, people have selective vision; when we look in a window, we focus on a specific

Figure 6 *Composition with Red, Blue, and Yellow* (1927) by the Dutch artist Piet Mondrian was among the earliest nonobjective or nonrepresentational works in Western art. Mondrian wanted to remove art from its mimetic (or descriptive) role to address spiritual concerns.

object and ignore the many reflections and distractions. That is why a camera records so much more visual information when it shoots through a window than we do when looking through the glass.

In some cases, realism becomes a form of *idealism*, the representation of the world not as it is but as it should be. An artist uses elements of realism, but erases the blemishes and flaws. Apply this idea to the Modesto Post Office mural in Figure 2. As discussed in Chapter 1, the artist ignored the Depression (so it is not an unbiased or objective reflection of reality) and painted an idealized and very successful farm.

Art historians also may distinguish between academic and nonacademic styles. An academic style tends to be orderly and systematic rather than radically experimental (that is, the art tends not to threaten accepted standards of beauty, technique, or subject). The history of art is characterized by confrontations between these two traditions, although the border between academic and nonacademic styles is fluid over time. When Claude Monet and other Impressionists began exhibiting their work in 1874, conservative French critics representing the interests of the academy claimed that art suffered irreparable damage from which it would never recover. Few people today view Impressionist painters as dangerous radicals.

Modernism developed outside the academy as artists experimented with new materials, new technologies, and new modes of representation, including an increased interest in nonobjective subjects. They were influenced by new theories of relativity (in optics, physics, and psychology, for example) that challenged their certainties or "truths" (the mechanics of sight; the nature of the universe and the composition of matter; the capacities of the human psyche) and questioned the visual conventions of representation. If what we see may not be "real," then how we do we know "reality?" In the 1950s, modernism's search for meaning and appropriate representation witnessed the elevation of formal and design considerations as the true subject of art and the debasement of anecdotal (narrative) imagery. By the last quarter of the twentieth century, these premises and constrictions had become canonical (authoritative). Postmodern considerations of appropriation (borrowing from other sources), the elevation of the commonplace, presentation (the reassessment of methodologies of exhibition), and globalization (assimilation and borderless culture) challenged modernist alienation.

Artists' Biographies

An artist's biography may seem to relate more to an historian than to an art historian, but the life experiences of artists are important in understanding and interpreting their works. The illness that affected Vincent van Gogh certainly played a significant role in his paintings from 1888 until his death in 1890. One cannot ignore the fact that the Baroque painter Artemisia Gentilleschi was raped when one discusses her many paintings of empowered women triumphant over men. In studying the *Greek Slave*, Hiram Powers's attitudes toward slavery as well as the location of his Florentine workshop (just a few blocks from the gallery in which Praxiteles's *Medici Venus* [http://harpy.uccs.edu/greek/sculpt/medici.jpg] was exhibited) guide us in our analysis. Even the very nonobjective work of Piet Mondrian's *Composition in Red, Yellow, and Blue* (1927) (Fig. 6) was a reaction to the post-World War I sense of loss.

World War I transformed society; the defining rules and the sense of order were shattered by the war's inhumanity. Advances in science that had promised to make life better had instead risen to new levels of destruction and barbarity. Mondrian believed that his art touched a chord deep within the human psyche that could not and should not be grounded in the false materialism of the tangible world. "Truth" existed outside and above the world of appearances. Paintings were the product of an inner creative force and not external vision; the visible world was not reality, only an illusion. His mature paintings were statements in primary colors intersected by black lines against a neutral white background far removed from the concerns of the material world.

We also can discuss the biography or life history of a work of art. We refer to this as its *provenance*. The provenance of a work includes: its original patrons; the reasons for its commission; its ownership trail; its maintenance (cleaning and restoration) record; and any anecdotes, stories, or critical essays associated with it. In 2001, an exhibit of paintings by the nineteenth-century American painter Winslow Homer focused not on his well-known Civil War images, not on the ruggedly individualistic Adirondack woodsmen and trappers, not on the sensitive images of newly freed African Americans, but on the critical response to his paintings from 1870 to 1880. Whereas audiences now may regard Homer's paintings with some nostalgia (a class in a one-room schoolhouse, boys playing snap-the-whip in a field at recess), Homer's contemporary critics rebuked him for his unsentimental objectivity, his elevation of mundane subjects, and his scumbled (rough) surfaces created by rapid (and somewhat messy) application of paint. The critical reception of Homer's work during the 1870s is part of the provenance or biography of each painting presented in the exhibition.

Technique, Process, and Media

When critics denounced the uneven surfaces, sloppy application of paint, and careless drawing of Homer's paintings, preferring the smooth finish, controlled brush, and careful sketching of his contemporaries in the United States, they were reacting to his technique rather than the content. The study and analysis of technique and process are twofold: the choice of materials used in the execution of a work and the manipulation of these materials. Taken together, they establish the characteristics of an artist's personal style, for example, the difference between Michelangelo and Winslow Homer.

Equally important is an understanding of the materials used by the artist. Every material has its strengths and weaknesses, and no artist can successfully force a material to perform beyond its capabilities. Clay is weaker than marble, so a terracotta sculpture cannot sustain the extensions into space of marble without some additional support. Similarly, marble is weaker than bronze. Artists must understand the essential or inherent properties of their materials as they conceptualize and realize the finished work. Art textbooks have illustrations of marble sculptures that are Roman copies of original Greek bronzes. While a bronze figure can balance on its thin ankles, a Roman artist copying the Greek work into weaker marble had to add a pillar or tree stump to stabilize the finished work. Notice in Figure 5 that Powers incorporated a drapery-wrapped post for support.

Changes in technology, applied materials, and applied science also influence the arts. A history of Western architecture can be written from the perspective of such changes. Classical (fifth-century) Athenian architects relied on a post and lintel system (vertical supports with a horizontal crossbar) in building. This technology was limited by the strength of marble. A marble beam or lintel could not span a wide space, forcing architects to place structural columns close together. Thus, there were few large uninterrupted interior spaces in which Athenian citizens could gather. A few centuries later, Roman architects borrowed arch technology from neighboring Near

Eastern builders and blended it with post and lintel construction, thus expanding their architectural language. Coupled with changes in applied materials (the use of concrete, for example, that could be poured in rubble-filled forms) the arch and its derivatives, the vault and dome, enabled Roman architects to span larger spaces and build uninterrupted interior halls. By the twelfth century, architects had modified the round-headed Roman arch to create the *ogival* or pointed Gothic arch and had developed an external skeletal system of flying buttresses to span higher and still larger spaces.

If we skim over seven centuries of architectural change and innovation and jump to nineteenth-century Chicago, we find another series of developments in building technology that sociologists suggest contributed to the growth of modern cities. The confluence of the devastating Chicago fire, the development of the Otis elevator, and the application of structural skeletons borrowed from bridge technology contributed to the birth of the skyscraper.

Similar histories can be written about changes in technique as the result of the shift from tempera (egg-based binder) to oil (oil-based binder) paints, from wood panels to canvas, from chalk and charcoal to graphite pencils, from etching to engraving, from canvas to computer screen and performance space. None of these changes should be construed as evolution and in no case did the older techniques disappear. Each change in technology added to the wealth of tools and possibilities available to artists to explore.

New media present a number of challenges to contemporary art historians and critics. Two authors who contributed to the modern understanding of the place of new media in modern society were Walter Benjamin and Marshall McLuhan.

Benjamin's pivotal essay, "Art in the Age of Mechanical Reproduction," was written the same year (1936) that Piet Mondrian, discussed above, published his essay on new painting. According to Benjamin, new media's ability to reproduce original works of art would liberate them from a single authentic (unique) meaning (or aura) and open them to a complex interweaving of meanings based on mass consumption and relocation. For Benjamin, the authority that historically identified works of art within specific cultural institutions and traditions would be replaced by a multiplicity of interpretations and contexts when that object (or sound) is reproduced, mass-produced, and distributed. Mechanically reproduced works of art, then, derive their power from their relocation within new and potentially ever-changing environments and their availability to new consumers within a mass culture. Unlike Mondrian, whose work was to carry a viewer beyond the mundane world, Benjamin placed art actively in the world. By challenging the singularity of a work of art, Benjamin both democratized and politically motivated it.

The impact of media on social systems was first discussed in 1967 in a groundbreaking book, *The Medium is the Message* by Marshall McLuhan. According to McLuhan, new media issues, including faster communication, borderless culture, and new collective experiences, would shape the late twentieth-century world. Viewers from the United States, Europe, and Africa could receive an image produced in India instantly and simultaneously. Messages travel faster, information travels faster, and the world becomes a global village.

Among the pioneers in video art was Nam June Paik. Paik recontextualized video, moving it from mainstream commercial or pop culture communication on intimate home television monitors to wall-mounted, multiple-monitor presentations in an art gallery. Using magnets and color synthesizers, he distorted and manipulated the imagery on the cathode ray tube (CRT) to explore variables in imagery and sound. Unlike the abstract representation of time in other two-dimensional and three-dimensional arts, video art relies on both the passage of real time as it is recorded and the experience of real time as it is played back. The audience, then, is aware of the collapse of the past (recording) into the present (watching).

In the 1990s, digital technology was added to the toolbox of artists' materials. The power to synthesize, manipulate, and construct a "virtual" reality changed the relationship of a viewer to an object. Because the object exists as coded information in a database, its substance or materiality is fluid rather than concrete.

Iconography and Iconology

Finally, there is iconography—the study of symbols an artist uses to convey meaning—and iconology—the study of the cultural context of those symbols. As suggested at the end of Chapter 1, artists rely on the viewer's ability to read and interpret the iconography or symbols as visual shorthand. Many of the interpretive models discussed above rely on the viewer's understanding of symbols. In Powers's *Greek Slave* (Fig. 5), the small cross on the post is read as a symbol of Christianity and Christian virtue. The farmer and his wife in the

Modesto Post Office (Fig. 2) represent Thomas Jefferson's yeoman (independent) farmer who, according to Jefferson, is the backbone of American values.

The late twentieth century was characterized by an increased globalism created by shifts in sociopolitical and economic considerations, increased communication through the Internet, the rapid transmission and dissemination of video imagery in popular media, and population mobility. It is not unusual to participate in an interactive Internet conference with panelists from India, China, the United States, South Africa, and an audience drawn from nearly every continent. This kind of global expansion, although it may share some aspects of earlier colonialism, promotes the growth of borderless societies. As such, it opens the door to an increasingly wider range of images, symbols, and models for artists to incorporate into their work and challenges the audience to expand its worldview.

TESTING YOUR SKILLS: LOOKING FOR MEANING

Select a painting, drawing, sculpture, or photograph and write down everything that comes to mind as you look at it. As discussed in Chapter 1, both careful observation and the careful recording of information are important steps in developing visual literacy skills. Again, do not edit, analyze, or prioritize what you observe. Do not be shy about noting both what you see and what you assume about the work you are looking at; you can discard irrelevant material later. Similar to your list from Chapter 1, this list will include both observable and associative data.

As you study your completed list, especially the associative information, you may notice that the data moves from immediate impressions (quickly seen and general) to inferences (slowly discovered and specific). Your list will help you answer the following questions. From your observations, what is the subject matter? Is there only one subject? Is there more than one possible interpretation? Finally, what role has the artist played in directing our attention to specific passages in the work we observed? The answer to this question is found in Chapter 3.

3
UNDERSTANDING FORMAL ELEMENTS

Beyond the questions of contextual and historical interpretation and stylistic analysis is the *formal analysis*. In a formal analysis, art historians examine the materials used by artists and the processes of construction. In the 1950s and 1960s, formal analysis was the dominant methodology followed by critics and historians; the subject or narrative content, crucial to the interpretative methodologies discussed in the previous chapter, was dismissed as kitsch.

How has an artist handled colors, lines, and shapes? How are space, mass, volume, and texture used by the artist? These categories and the way in which an artist organizes them make up the formal language of art. Design principles, the organization of formal elements by the artist, will be discussed in Chapter 4. The formal elements used by an artist can be compared to the words and phrases used by a writer, while the design principles are the grammar.

COLOR

Colors are refracted wavelengths of light that exist in a bonded relationship. In the late seventeenth century, the English physicist and mathematician Sir Isaac Newton developed one of the earliest color charts to demonstrate the relationships or bonds between colors. His knowledge of color came not only from the close observation of nature, especially the rainbow, but also from the observation that white light, passing through a prism, broke apart into separate bands of color called the *spectrum*. When he bounced the spectrum bands through a second prism, they rejoined to become a single beam of white light. Just as the prism refracted (broke apart) light into its components, wavelengths of light are either absorbed by or reflected from an object. A red apple (that may have hit Newton on the head) reflects the longest spectrum wavelength, which we call red, while absorbing the remaining wavelengths. Pigments used by an artist similarly reflect or absorb specific wavelengths. Newton created a circular chart or *color wheel* to record colors and display their relationships to one another. Although there have been other systems introduced in the West over the more than three hundred years since Newton developed his color wheel, they would have been impossible without his pioneering work in color theory.

Color Terms

Hue: a synonym for color. Each hue is determined by its wavelength and has a specific position on the color wheel.

Primary Colors: hues that cannot be made from other colors. For pigment, they are red, yellow, and blue. The primary colors in light (used in photography, computer graphics, and video) are red, green, and blue-violet (hence, a computer monitor is listed as RGB).

Secondary Colors: hues made by mixing two primary colors. They are, for pigment, orange (red plus yellow), green (blue plus yellow), and violet (red plus blue).

Tertiary Colors: also called intermediate colors. Mixing a primary color with a secondary color makes these hues.

Analogous Colors: colors next to one another on the color wheel because they share a common hue.

Complementary Colors: colors directly opposite one another on the color wheel that do not share any common hues, such as red and green. Placing complementary colors side by side in a painting intensifies each, especially at the edges.

Neutrals: black and white. The Mu Qi ink painting *Six Persimmons* (Fig. 7) is a very subtle use of the neutrals.

Value: the relationship of light to dark that helps define a hue or color. We divide value into *tints* that reflect more light to the eye and *shades* that appear darker because less light is reflected. How bright

Figure 7 *Six Persimmons* by Southern Song (Chinese) painter Mu Qi is a detail of a hanging scroll in the Ryoukouin at the Daitokuji Buddhist Temple complex in Kyoto, Japan. The painting is used as a focal point in Zen (Chan) meditation.

or dull a color appears also may be called its *intensity* or its *saturation*. A hue that reflects more light, such as yellow, has a greater value and a greater intensity than a hue that absorbs more light, such as violet. This also helps determine color placement on the color wheel, so that yellow should always be at the top and violet at the bottom. A *value scale* records the transition from light to dark from the neutral colors white (highest value) and black (lowest value). There are traditionally seven levels between white and black; a color said to be of medium intensity or value is in the middle position.

The selection of colors used by an artist is called a *palette*. The term palette also refers to the surface or board on which an artist places selected pigments and on which these pigments are mixed. We can speak about *warm palettes* that are heavy on the reds, oranges, and yellows, and *cool palettes* dominated by greens, blues, and violets. These color families also carry symbolic meanings; we associate the warm colors with fire, sunshine, and anger, whereas the cool colors remind us of water and the sky. Artists also may limit their palettes to only a single hue, although the values may cover the entire value scale. In that case, we talk about a *monochromatic palette*. Pablo Picasso's large canvas *Guernica* (http://grnica.swinternet.cp.uk) is a monochromatic canvas that uses only the gray scale. This special palette is called a *grisaille*. When an artist uses multiple hues as well as multiple values, the work is *polychromatic,* as in the Modesto, California post office mural (Fig. 2).

Colors are used descriptively (the green of a ripe Pippin apple), sometimes called local color, symbolically (white to represent purity for a modern Western bride), and psychologically (the calming effect of a subtle rose tint in a waiting room). Think of the number of common phrases that equate emotional or psychological states to specific colors. As an example, let us consider the word "blue." How many ways can we understand this one simple word? After all, this is one of the earliest colors we learn to identify. The sky is blue; the water is blue; blueberries are blue; even bubblegum-flavored ice cream may be blue. But, are they all the same blue? How do we know what blue is meant when someone uses the term to describe an object? While there is a shared understanding that aids us in determining and communicating meaning in the above examples, each of us will envision a slightly different blue based on personal experience.

What if we should say, "The man is blue." Does this mean the same thing as "The water is blue."? If we were Hindi, the sentence could mean the same thing. The god Krishna is painted as a blue man to indicate his darker complexion. This, along with the context of the painting, helps to distinguish Krishna from other deities within the Hindu pantheon. Similarly, if we referred to an individual whose body temperature had dropped significantly below normal, we might say that the individual had turned blue, indicating a dangerous hypothermia. However, for most people the sentence ("The man is blue.") means something quite different. Blue, in this context, indicates a mood rather than a color. We use this term to indicate a mild depression, a psychological state rather than a physical one. At times, these meanings may merge. The twentieth-century painter Pablo Picasso went through a "Blue period" early in his career, after the suicide of his closest friend Casagemas, coupled with his sense of alienation (both as a Spaniard living in Paris and as a painter outside the established gallery marketplace). During this period, Picasso's palette tended to the blues, as did his mood; his subjects included individuals who were suffering—the blue guitarist who could only play sad songs on his blue guitar, the haggard features of a life-worn woman ironing—or living on the fringes of normative society. After a year, with a new dealer, a new mistress, and a new feeling of inclusion, Picasso emerged from his depression and entered what has popularly been called the "Rose (or Circus) period." His palette brightened and his subject matter emphasized life through the harlequins of the circus. Similarly, in popular music Billie Holiday sang "the blues," a style characterized by lyrics of struggle and by "blue notes" that are a key to the sound of the blues themselves.

When artists use blue in a painting, all of these issues become a part of its meaning; it is the viewer's responsibility to determine which of the many definitions or meanings is/are most suitable. In determining meaning, the observant interpreter begins to deconstruct or "unpack" the clues. How is blue used? Is it descriptive, as the blue eyes in a portrait? Is it symbolic, as in Toni Morrison's novel *The Bluest Eye*? Are there specific cultural links, as the blue of Krishna or the blue note "scales" in western Africa?

Color choices are dependent on both availability and cultural practice. Contemporary palettes have grown larger with the addition of more saturated chemical (synthetic) pigments rather than the often more subtle natural pigments. Ndebele women in the Transvaal of South Africa (http://www.ux1.eiu.edu/~cfrb/painted-houses.htm) north of Pretoria, traditionally have painted their houses each year with images drawn from the surrounding plains. After the middle of the twentieth century, as more synthetic house paint became available, their murals have become bolder and brighter.

The naming of colors as well as their symbolic meaning is culturally determined. During the European Middle Ages and Renaissance, colors were associated with specific organs and fluids in the body that in turn determined one's personality and temperament: black for melancholy, yellow for churlishness, green for apathy, and red for optimism. Many of these references have remained as part of Western folk culture, as when we say someone is "green with envy."

Essential to art theory in India is the concept of *rasa* or inner essence. Like the Medieval and Renaissance humours discussed above, each *rasa* refers to an emotional state which in turn is identified both with a particular God within the pantheon and a specific color. The God Krishna was mentioned during the discussion of the color blue; Krishna and the color blue are both identified with the *rasa* love. Knowledge of color symbolism is important in understanding different cultural traditions. We would be out of place if we wore black (a Western tradition) rather than white (an Asian tradition) to a Chinese funeral.

If in doubt, always turn to a dictionary for help. James Pierce's *From Abacus to Zeus* (Prentice Hall, 2001) and James Hall, *A Dictionary Subjects and Symbols in Art* (Icon Editions/Harper Row, 1979) are two of the most frequently cited texts and are helpful with Western symbolism. The *Dictionary of Symbols* by John Tresidder (Chronicle Books, 1998) and the *Illustrated Dictionary of Symbols in Eastern and Western Art* (Icon Editions/Harper Row, 1996) by James Hall are broader in scope and can answer simple questions about Asian and African cultures. More specialized symbol dictionaries have been published on specific culture areas and groups. These should be available in your library and online.

LINE

A line is the visible record of a moving point. Like color, line can be both descriptive and symbolic. They are part of the way in which we understand and describe our world. We can describe lines as *mechanical* (straight and machine-like, such as those in Mondrian's painting reproduced in Fig. 6), *organic* (flowing and curving, such as those used by the Western Arnhem Land artist to describe the Emu in Fig. 3) and *calligraphic* (varying in thickness, as we find in the persimmon stems in Mu Qi's ink painting in Fig. 7). Various kinds of lines have acquired symbolic meaning: vertical lines for strength (a soldier standing at attention or a tree), horizontal lines as resting (a sleeping person), curved and diagonal lines for movement as in the upward thrust of the curving arms of *Expansion I* (1999) by W. Scott Trimble (Fig. 8). A *contour line* defines the edges of forms. These edges may be drawn as actual lines as we see in the Emu in Figure 3 or implied lines where two colors meet as, for example, in the Boynton mural (Fig. 2).

Compositional lines both define forms, move viewers' eyes from action to action or subject to subject, and organize the surface. Often compositional lines are implied and not actually drawn. In Hiram Powers's *Greek Slave*, our eyes follow the downward glance of the captive's eyes, although the artist has not placed any lines there. One of the most important implied lines is between a physical work of art (in any media) and the viewer. The power of these lines helps hold our attention; in figural work (work with a human subject), this line is often through the eyes. Look again at Stuart's portrait of Washington (Fig. 4). On whom do Washington's eyes focus?

SHAPE AND SPACE

A shape is a defined or limited area created by real or implied contour lines. In sculpture or architecture, shape is defined by the physical edge of the work; in two-dimensional work, contour lines or the meeting of two or more colors, values, or textures create edges. We divide shapes into *geometric* or *rectilinear* shapes (circles, triangles, or squares) and *biomorphic* or *organic* shapes (as found in nature). On a flat plane (paintings, drawings, photographs, and prints), a shape has width and height. In space (sculpture and architecture), a shape has width, height, and depth defined as *mass* (shapes that have solidity) and *volume* (shapes that displace space). In paintings, drawings, and prints, mass and volume are implied by the careful use of shading. In photographs, the careful placement or use of light suggests mass and volume. Shapes also can be described as *positive* (the actual shape of an object and limited or defined by its contour lines) and *negative* (the voids formed between the shapes).

Figure 8 The upraised arms of W. Scott Trimble's *Expansion I* (1999) work within its site to emphasize the stands of redwood trees in the surrounding grove. The patina (surface colors and textures) will age and change over time as the metal reacts with the environment.

Space is both the physical areas around or between shapes and the illusion of depth on a flat surface. Artists create the perception of a three-dimensional world using techniques of *perspective*. Many perspective systems can be used to describe space on a two-dimensional surface.

The illusion of space can be created by the use of *aerial* or *atmospheric perspective* in which distant objects become less distinct and their colors more muted, whereas close objects have crisper edges and clearer hues. *Scientific* or *linear perspective* is a mathematical system developed during the Renaissance using diminishing *scale* (relative size) to achieve the illusion of space that has remained an important method through which Western-trained artists order or systematically arrange space. As objects recede in space, they appear smaller than objects close at hand. An artist begins by creating a *horizon line* with one or more *vanishing points* from which radiating lines or *orthogonals* will be drawn. We can see this in the furrows behind the farmer in the Modesto mural (Fig. 2).

Other traditional methodologies for ordering space include systems of *overlapping* (layering shapes), *position* (shapes higher or lower on the picture plane), *convergence* (decreasing size of shape as it recedes), and *relative scale* (the relationship of large to small shapes). These systems can also be seen in Mu Qi's painting *Six Persimmons* from the first half of the thirteenth century (Fig. 7), which, despite its title, is not about persimmons at all but about Buddhist precepts and their interrelationships. Mu Qi places each persimmon in an ambiguous space on the hanging scroll. The three persimmons on the left form a diagonal that appears to move forward from the background space, with the middle persimmon in the group slightly overlapping the one behind. Similarly, the far right persimmon is partially obscured by the persimmon to its immediate left. The relationship between the remaining persimmons is ambiguous. Mu Qi also subtly modulates the quality of the ink to further suggest their spatial relationships.

No matter what perspective system an artist follows, all suggest a *foreground* (the front edge of the canvas or paper), a *middle ground*, and a *background* (that often appears to flow infinitely into the distance). These methods create an *implied space*, because the actual surface of the canvas or paper is relatively flat.

In sculpture, space is tangible. A sculpture exists in real or *positive space* and sculptural extensions (whether actual or implied) continue spatial control beyond the central mass or core, as we see in

Trimble's work (Fig. 8). The area surrounding and defined by the sculpture and the open areas within the central mass of the sculpture are called *negative space*. It is active and tangible although there is nothing physical in the space. The open space between the thrusting forms of Trimble's work psychologically enclose and define the space, just as the space serves to delineate the forms themselves. For this reason, when we approach a sculpture in a museum or public space, we feel its presence and power when we are still some distance from the actual object.

Go once more to Figure 5, *Greek Slave*, to see how Hiram Powers used space. Judging from the angle of the shot, the photographer was standing just to the figure's right and shooting straight on. From this view, the woman looks away from us and the chains are emphasized. But Powers did not carve a closed form (a form that does not move in space). Rather, this image is open in form (it twists and moves through space). Why can we say this? First, Powers has shifted the weight of his subject (*contrapposto* or counterbalancing) so that more of her body weight centers her left foot (planted firmly on the ground) than on her right (where the weight is on the balls of her foot with a raised heel). Her bent right leg implies movement that is reinforced by the displacement in her hips and the slight diagonal position of her shoulders. She balances herself on the pillar to her right (see the palm of her right hand), while the left arm moves forward so that her hand covers her pudenda. Would we see something different if the photographer had chosen a different position from which to shoot? Would the chains be more or less important if the photographer had moved to the right and shot from the sculpture's left? In that case, the manacled woman's face would hold our attention as she looked down at us. The distance (space) between our gaze and her gaze would be more active (see the discussion above of negative and positive space). In the current photograph, we are looking at her and she is looking away from us; from the alternate vantage point suggested above, we would be looking at one another. What would happen if we saw her from the back? Would she appear to be walking away from us? What significant information would be lost if we only saw her from the back?

Paintings and works on paper use negative space, as do relief carvings such as the gateways at the Temple at Sanchi (Fig. 1). The spaces between forms on the surface, discussed as negative and positive spaces above, work together spatially on the flat surface plane to create the illusion of negative and positive space.

The way an artist manipulates color on a surface also creates spatial references. Go back to the painting by Piet Mondrian (Fig. 6) and look at the colors on the surface. The more intense blue at the bottom of the canvas appears to recede, creating a hole in the surface, while the yellow on the painting's right edge advances. Examine the black lines. Are they above or below the large central square? What is the relationship of the horizontal line at the top to the red module? Does it bisect a rectangle or are there two distinctly outlined, stacked red quadrangles? What happens where the lines cross? The illusion of space in Mondrian's *Composition in Red, Blue, and Yellow* is very subtle.

A very active space, similar to the stage in a theater, is used by performance artists. In the twentieth century, a number of artists moved away from traditional media to explore performance spaces. Performance artists interact with their spaces and their audiences as if they were living sculptures. As in an analysis of video and digital media, performance artists work with real time rather than the illusion of time and within real space, rather the illusion of space. We will discuss this in relation to the artist Ann Hamilton later in the chapter.

TEXTURE AND SURFACE

Texture includes both the physical (actual) and the implied surface of a work. We have already discussed the critical response to the physical surfaces of Winslow Homer's paintings. Paint on the surface of the Mondrian has crackled with age. One is aware of the *actual texture* of the surface and may discuss the quality of the paint on a surface (dry, moist, thick, thin, etc.) and the tactility of the surface itself (wood, metal, paper, cloth, marble, clay, etc). But artists also use *invented* or *implied textures* that are meant to simulate and recall real textures. A still-life painting is a complex interplay of implied textures (glass, wood, metal, flowers, fruits, leaves, insects, and cloth). Objects in still-life paintings by the nineteenth-century American artist William Harnett (http://www.huntington.org/ArrtDiv/HarnettPict.html) are so realistic in their appearance that they trick us into believing they are real and not painted, a process called *trompe l'oeil* or fool the eye.

Sculpture may use both actual and implied textures. Works by the nineteenth-century French sculptor August Rodin (http://www.rodinmuseum.org) carry the imprint of his fingers and tools; they have lively actual surfaces as compared to the polished surfaces of *Greek Slave* (Fig. 2). Hiram Powers, however, has implied the textures of the cloth hanging on the post (even differentiating the cloth from its fringes), her flesh and hair, the metallic cross, and links of chain.

Some surface textures are not the result of the artist's direct manipulation of the surface, but are part of the natural aging process of the work itself. Artists working with public sculpture must consider how their work will age with exposure to sun and rain and the patinas (surfaces) that will develop. The textures of the weathered surface of Trimble's *Expansion I* (Fig. 8) will change over time from oxidation of the metals.

Artists may combine actual and implied textures in *collages* (on a two-dimensional surface) and *assemblages*, a sculpture constructed from a variety of materials with many textures. When analyzing collages (for example, the paper collages by the African American artist Romare Bearden [http://www.beardenfoundation.org/]) and assemblages (as in the work of the Native American artist Jimmie Durham), the relationship between the actual and implied surface textures is part of the meaning.

TIME AND MOTION

Time and motion are implied in paintings, sculpture, photographs, and drawings. They form part of the invisible world discerned by Perkins's hungry or intelligent eye that was discussed in the introduction.

In many cultures, as well as in twentieth-century Western art, time and motion are integral aspects of the work. An African mask like the *Efe Gelede* (Fig. 9) is not encountered as a static image within its own culture; it is dynamically presented with costume, music, dance, and song as it celebrates the mythical power of women in Nigerian Yoruba society. The static display of the mask in a museum rather than the performance of that mask *in situ* strips it of power and meaning. A discussion of the mask using Western formulas of formal analysis yields little real information about the work. In a museum environment, we see and thus describe the mask using a methodology and vocabulary alien to Yoruba culture.

The twentieth century found Western artists breaking away from established media and expectations to explore new media and techniques. Art as spectacle and performance has moved in and out

Figure 9 As part of a festival to honor the role and power of women in Yoruba (Nigeria) society, the *Efe Gelede* mask appears in the marketplace at dusk to prepare and transform the secular economic sphere into a sacred site in which the world of people and the world of the *orishas* (ancestors and deities) will meet.

of the history of Western art for hundreds of years. In the fifteenth century, the Renaissance architect Filippo Brunelleschi designed a network of cables used in the Duomo or Cathedral of Florence (Santa Maria Del Fiore) to enable performers to fly; a similar system of cables designed by the twentieth-century American architect Phillip Johnson for the Crystal Cathedral in Southern California allows performer-angels to fly during the Christmas pageant. The *Happenings* of the 1960s, building on a half century of performance art, moved art off gallery walls and into real space, away from the implied (the representation of a person or object in motion) and into the actual (live action), away from contained works (in a frame or closed form) to open forms.

In the 1980s and 1990s, performances and multimedia installations continued to blur the boundaries between theater and other visual/aural art traditions. The performance artist Ann Hamilton and the video artist Bill Viola engulf the viewer in sensory experiences based in reality. Many of Hamilton's installations focus on events or people overlooked by earlier historians, such as domestic workers or nonstriking factory and field labor. The 1991 installation *indigo blue* (Fig. 10) was commissioned by the Spoleto (U.S.A.) Festival in Charleston, South Carolina as part of a series of installations on the theme of Charleston history. As she so often does in her work, Hamilton chose an abandoned workers' space that carried, because of its address, the traces (or memories—see our earlier discussion of Derrida in Chapter 2) of forgotten historical events. In *indigo blue*, the street address carries the name of the woman (Eliza Pinkney) who introduced the plant indigo (the source of a rich blue African dye that is also called indigo) that became a major source of Charleston's economic power in the eighteenth and early nineteenth centuries. Indigo dye was commonly used on workmen's clothing, which is why we call them blue-collar workers. In the photograph that documents the installation, you can see, behind the performer at the table, a pallet of stacked, folded work clothes. The person at the table is erasing passages from a history book, symbolizing the anonymity of the workers (men) who would have worn the shirts and trousers as well as the unnamed workers (women) who laundered and ironed them. *indigo blue* also addresses issues of identity (implying power) in history (Eliza Pinkney) and historically anonymity (and therefore powerless—the repair shop and domestic workers). Unless we attend a performance such as *indigo blue* or experience an installation, we know these works only through docu-

Figure 10 *indigo blue* (1991) by Ann Hamilton was among eighteen works in the extended exhibition "Places with a Past" in Charleston, South Carolina. Her three-part, two-room installation addressed the dichotomy between history as fact or event and history as memory and experience.

mentation. We miss the physical environment of the work—the smell of the clothes, the sound of the erasures, the dampness of the room, and so forth. Similar to the museum experience of an African mask, our appreciation of performance or installation work is, therefore, limited. This is true even if the work has been recorded on video; we watch, but remain alienated or distanced from the experience. Compare your experience listening to music at a concert to hearing the same music on a compact disk or watching a play versus reading it. How many additional senses are involved in the actual experience?

TESTING YOUR SKILLS: UNDERSTANDING FORMAL ELEMENTS

As suggested in the final section of the previous chapter, we can only improve our visual skills if we practice using them. Write down each of the formal elements discussed in this chapter. Find an object or image and, as you did in the previous chapters, carefully observe it, looking for the individual elements we have discussed. Your list will help you remember them. Write down all your observations without editing or prioritizing. Be as specific as possible. For example, as you describe the color of an object, ask yourself if it is really "just red" or if there are tonal subtleties. If specific formal elements (such as color) evoke distinct memories or responses, write these down as well.

Once you have completed your list, ask yourself the following question. How has the artist's manipulation of the formal elements added meaning to the work? This is the subject of the next chapter.

4

PRINCIPLES OF DESIGN
AND COMPOSITION

Once the content and medium of a work have been determined, an artist begins to order or organize the composition. To do this, an artist relies on a body of design principles.

BALANCE

Balance creates a sense of harmony or equilibrium by evenly distributing the visual weight. This can be accomplished in a number of ways, including the repetition of colors or lines, the reiteration of shapes, or the introduction of mathematical principles such as the Greek "golden section." Chapter 3 discussed how an artist creates the illusion of three-dimensional space on a two-dimensional plane through the use of a vantage-point from which *orthogonals* or lines radiate; this center focal point produces a *radial* balance from which all other aspects of the work appear to project outward. With *bilateral* or *axial symmetrical*, the left and right sides of a work appear as mirror or near mirror images. The Yoruba artist who carved the *Efe Gelede* mask (Fig. 9) provides a confident and graceful axial balance of color and form. Sometimes called *bilateral symmetry*, its overuse can lead to an unexciting image if not handled deftly. Shifting symmetry slightly away from the mirror image of bilateral symmetry is called *approximate symmetry*. When the right and left sides of a composition do not reflect one another but are equally weighted visually, it is called *asymmetrical balance*. With asymmetrical balance, the sense of equilibrium is maintained through a careful manipulation of shapes, values, and color. Artists play with symmetry and balance to add visual excitement to their works. Mondrian's *Composition in Red, Blue, and Yellow* (Fig. 6) achieves its balance not only through the judicious placement of colored squares but also mathematically by reflecting the external proportions of the canvas itself in the dimensions of the internal red square.

DOMINANCE AND SUBORDINATION

In addition to issues of symmetry and balance, artists are conscious of the consequences of dominance and subordination in which some elements are stressed while others are not. With too much equally weighted information, a viewer may have difficulty distinguishing the most important elements in a work.

SCALE AND PROPORTION

Included in any discussion of dominance and subordination is scale and proportion, the relationships among components of a work. Scale (the work's relationship to external forces) and proportion (a work's internal relationships) are not absolute but reflect cultural norms. The mathematically ideal proportions of the human figure in Western aesthetics has undergone a number of changes since the its introduction more than twenty-five hundred years ago. We need only to look at the changes in the presentation of the human figure in Western advertising over the past twenty years—from the malnourished, anorexic images of waiflike models of the 1980s to the slightly fuller (although still thin) models of the late 1990s—to see these changes. In this context, human proportion is an aspect of cultural concepts of beauty. Compare the image of Powers's *Greek Slave* (Fig. 5) to that of the *yakshi* (fertility figure) that forms the bracket on the Sanchi gateway (Fig. 1).

Scale, like proportion, is relative. A one-foot object appears quite large in comparison to a one-inch object, yet very small compared to a ten-foot object. If we look at the reproduction in an art textbook, we will discover that the prehistoric sculpture of the *Venus of Willendorf* (http://vienna.cc/english/nhmuseum2.htm) appears to be as large as Michelangelo's sculpture of the biblical *David* (http://www.arca.nct/db/musei/accadem.htm). Yet, *Venus* fits comfortably in the palm of your hand and *David* is three times lifesize. Scale, then, is determined contextually. Imagine a dollhouse photographed against a blank background. Without visual clues to establish size, we would assume it was a standard house for human occupation. Now imagine the same dollhouse photographed in a child's playroom. Set against other toys in the room, it is clearly not habitable.

Artists manipulate scale and proportion to communicate specific ideas. Enlarging an object or subject beyond its natural scale increases its dominance while miniaturizing makes it more intimate (subordinate) and therefore more manageable. In 1986, the Neo-Dada artist Jeff Koons translated a mylar rabbit balloon into the stainless steel sculpture, *Rabbit* (1986) (http://broadartfoundation.org/collection/koons.html). At its normal size, a silver mylar balloon is a child's toy; a stainless steel rabbit over three feet tall is not only more imposing, but also more menacing.

REPETITION AND RHYTHM

Repetition and rhythm, created by repeating shapes colors, patterns, or lines help move the eye through a work. A composition is either *open* (moving out from the center) or *closed* (moving into a central core). By carefully balancing open and closed forms, our eyes will flow from the *focal point* of a work out to its edges and back in again. If one dominates the other, our eyes either fly off the surface (and we move away from the work because we are not attracted to it) or focus too narrowly on a few details.

A careful, yet unexpected, manipulation of open and closed forms can also add visual excitement to a finished work. Late-nineteenth-century artists such as Edgar Degas were fascinated by the edges in documentary photographs because they carried important contextual information. In many of his paintings, Degas forces the viewer to look at his edges: subjects walk off the edge, ballerinas are cut off by the edge, action continues off the edge. By working with active edges in this way, Degas suggests that the world is larger than the scene on the canvas. You can apply this to many visual media. If you look at a film produced before the age of video reproduction, you will see much less centering of imagery and much more important information on the edges than is common on more recent videos that are shot to comply with television specifications.

UNITY AND VARIETY

Too much information can be as confusing as too little. Artists strive to achieve an *economy of means* that eliminates all nonessential information. A careful reduction to the communicative essence of a work was an ideal of the middle of the twentieth-century *nonobjective* artists, for whom the formal elements of art were the subject matter.

The careful balance of formal elements and basic design principles creates *unity*, a sense of completeness or oneness in a work of art. A well-balanced work in which the components are integrated looks and feels "right." If there is a queasy feeling of imbalance, the work suffers. Piet Mondrian once said that he placed a finished painting on an easel at the foot of his bed at night before going to sleep so that it would be the first thing he saw in the morning. If it looked whole when he first saw it, he knew it was done; if not, he continued to work on it.

As with so many other "rules" about art, this, too, is not unbreakable. Artists consciously bend rules to achieve specific effects, such as temporality or impermanence and instability.

TESTING YOUR SKILLS: PRINCIPLES OF DESIGN AND COMPOSITION

As suggested at the end of the last chapter, we improve our visual skills through practice. Write down each of the basic principles of design discussed in this chapter. Find an object or image and, as you did in the previous chapters, carefully observe it. Look for the specific principles of design we discussed in this chapter. A list will help you remember them. Write down all your observations without editing or prioritizing. Be as specific as possible. Based on your observation, how has the artist guided your eyes to specific points in the work? Why?

5
APPLYING ART HISTORY'S TOOLS

Most of you have been sitting in a darkened classroom viewing slides and videos. But to truly understand how to approach a work of art, it is important to experience the real thing. Reproductions, no matter how beautiful they are, cannot substitute for an original work. As suggested in Chapter 4, photographs of sculpture cannot adequately convey scale and proportion. Sculpture, as well, has mass and volume. The way a work relates to its space and the multiple viewpoints that define its form cannot be appreciated from a photograph, even from a series of photographs. Rarely is the back of the *Venus of Willendorf* or multiple views of Michelangelo's *David* reproduced in a textbook. For that reason, an instructor may require a visual analysis of a work in a local museum or gallery that not only demonstrates your ability to process and apply the basic vocabulary and methodology of art history but provides, as well, a personal experience.

A visual analysis is similar to a position paper; it requires that we present and support our own ideas rather than those of a published scholar. In this case, rather than depend on what someone else says about a work of art, we must rely on our own eyes and come to our own conclusions. A careful analysis balances the presentation of formal elements with contextual information. In Figure 4, Gilbert Stuart's handling of the brush, his application of paint, his choice of color, and his manipulation of space might form part of a formal analysis. This discussion would inform a reader about Stuart's abilities as a painter, but it provides very little information about his sitter. The application of paint on the surface and the formal choices made by Stuart in this portrait were not his only concerns. Gilbert Stuart was interested in capturing a likeness of the sitter, including a sense of the sitter's personality. To limit our discussion to the formal elements, while an interesting design exercise, is therefore incomplete. When we look at the portrait of Washington, what is the first thing we notice? Is it the paint on the surface we see or is it the way in which his eyes engage us in a conversation?

A visual analysis can be not only an independent essay on a single work but also an essay that compares and contrasts two or more works by either the same or different artists, or part of a biographical or historical research paper. Gilbert Stuart painted more than one portrait of George Washington and his contemporaries in the Philadelphia-based Peale family painted many as well. Visual analyses of each of Stuart's portraits or of the Peale portraits would form the basis for a comparative paper. A biography of Stuart might use multiple visual studies to trace or establish his style. A history of Washington might include an examination of the many different portraits and how each represents changes in his public and political life.

PREPARING FOR YOUR ASSIGNMENT

An immediate reaction to a museum assignment/visual analysis may be pure terror. How can I do this? How will I know what work to choose when I get to the museum or gallery? I am not an art historian! First, relax. You are not alone. You share this moment of panic with many of your classmates. Your instructor does not expect you to have a paper that reads like that of a professional art historian or critic. So, choose a museum, wear comfortable shoes, and plan your visit (a bit of advance planning will make the experience less overwhelming). Your instructor may have narrowed the assignment for you by providing a list of acceptable works or a series of specific rooms to visit. If not, and if you live in a city with a large collection, spend some preparation time looking at the illustrations in your textbook to decide which stylistic period you want to study. Are you interested in French Post-Impressionism (Vincent van Gogh or Paul Cézanne) or, perhaps, American Abstract Expressionism (Jackson Pollock and Mark Rothko)? Since many museums have Internet sites, you should familiarize yourself with a large museum by look-ing at its website. The website will also provide the museum's sched-ule, fees, and address. Always carry your student identification card because most museums have special entrance fees for students. A website also will tell you if there are specific days in a museum's schedule when entrance fees are waived.

VISITING THE MUSEUM

Once you arrive, walk through the museum (or specific gallery in a large museum) and look at the works on exhibit. If you prepared for the assignment by visiting the museum's website, you may want to go directly to the work you saw online. If you choose to do this, notice the placement of the work within its exhibition space. Ask yourself if the work is different from what you expected to see based on your website experience.

Unless you are visiting a traveling show that has a specific entrance and exit, there is no right or wrong way to walk through a museum. Do not immediately fret over the assignment; first enjoy the experience. You do not have to stop and look at everything on exhibit (unless your assignment specified this). Wander through the museum's galleries and engage in a series of casual conversations with various works. Take notes as you walk around. As a work catches your fancy, write down its title, the artist, and its location in the gallery or museum so that you can come back to it. You might also want to take a few notes on what first attracted you to the piece (was it the size? the color? the story? the style?).

After you have walked through the museum, go back to the pieces that first caught your attention. One by one, ask yourself what drew you initially to the work and if you still are attracted to it. If the work no longer interests you, delete it and move to the next work on your list. Finally, choose one of the remaining works for your paper.

BEGINNING YOUR ANALYSIS

You are going to engage in an extended conversation with the work you have chosen (or perhaps *it* chose you!). Like all good conversa-tions, this one will include a series of questions and a set of responses. And, like good conversations, you must be an attentive "listener." You are about to "interview" a painting or sculpture.

All good interviewers come prepared with basic questions that they will ask the interviewee. Part of the preparatory planning for your museum visit should include a list of questions that you want to ask. These may include:

- What is the name of the artist?
- What is the work's title? Is the title descriptive or metaphoric? If the work in untitled, do not provide a title. The artist was not being lazy. It is not uncommon for works in the middle of the twentieth century to be untitled. The artist did not want to limit your ability to discover personal ideas in the work. If the work has a title, does the title help you to uncover the meaning beyond its immediate subject? Remember, a work has both subject (immediate appearance) and content (meaning).
- What is the work's date and stylistic period? How are they significant in understanding the work?
- What is the work's medium? An artist from the twentieth century may have used many media in a single work.
- What is the work's size? The relationship of the scale or size of a work to you as the viewer is an important part of the piece. Small works are much more intimate than monumental ones.
- What is the work's subject? This may be more difficult to discover in nonobjective works such as the Piet Mondrian discussed in Figure 6. In some nonrepresentational works, the subject may be the interrelationship of the principles of design and formal elements.
- What is the work's content? Remember, subject and meaning (content) are often different, even in nonobjective works. Refer back to the discussion of the portrait of Washington by Gilbert Stuart. The subject is "a portrait of an elderly man named George Washington" but its content is much more complex because of the symbolic meanings attached to Washington.

You may find it helpful not only to write down the basic questions that you want to ask, but to list elements of formal analysis (color, line, shape, space, texture, time, and motion) and basic design principles (balance, symmetry, unity). One way to make sure you cover everything is to write each element of analysis and design as a heading on your notepad. Thoroughly examine one characteristic at a time and write down what you discover on the page with that heading. As you complete each category, move on to the next. You may also want to sketch the work, purchase a postcard in the bookstore, or, if the museum permits, take a photograph. Do not rely on your memory; it is always better to write down a detailed description.

Interpretive methodologies and formal elements of art historical analysis are objective. But there is a final analysis that is more subjective and personal. What does the work say *to you*? What is your assessment of the work? This might include the notes you took concerning what initially attracted you to the work.

After you have written comments and observations about your chosen work, step back and look around the gallery in which it is exhibited. Artworks in museums borrow from the works surrounding them. Perhaps the museum has arranged the room chronologically or by style or by school (a group of artists with similar ideas). Perhaps the gallery concentrates on a single artist or family. After the curator has determined a theme for a specific exhibit or gallery, exhibit designers stage the works, focus the lighting, and arrange the exhibit. Consider the environment and write down your impressions.

Curators are conscious that the choices they make in mounting an exhibition shape the perceptions of museum visitors, especially when visitors are presented with new works or works from other cultures. That visitors assume a museum defines taste (beautiful/ugly), authenticity (art/not art), value (good/bad), and power (important/ unimportant) concerns contemporary curators. A 1999 exhibit at the Housatonic Museum of Art in Connecticut, *Producing Histories*, explored the way African art acquires meaning through display conventions, an idea we touched on in the brief discussion of the Yoruba *Efe Gelede* mask from Nigeria. The curator, Lyneise Williams, divided the museum into three primary galleries, each following a different exhibition convention. To create a consistent comparative base, she exhibited three almost identical Nigerian images from the Igbo people, one in each setting. The first gallery was organized around display conventions that Williams saw in the homes of collectors and that can be seen on popular television programs such as *Frasier*. In this gallery, pieces were set against typical home furnishings—a sofa, end and coffee tables, and a television set. The works become decorative elements and conversation pieces within a domestic setting. A second gallery explored the conventions of museum display, with works isolated on special pedestals, carefully lit, with informational labels and wall-mounted photographs to establish context. Each piece gains in stature as the representative of an entire culture. The final gallery recreates a museum storeroom in which pieces are shelved until needed. A museum visitor could then see the way setting influences understanding. The sculpture in the storehouse carried much less importance than the similar piece positioned in the carefully lit gallery. On a coffee table in a personal space, the sculpture became both an intriguing curio or souvenir of Africa and a statement about the collector and the process of collecting.

TESTING YOUR SKILLS: APPLYING ART HISTORY'S TOOLS

The visual literacy skills you practiced in the previous chapters will be applied to your museum assignment. This chapter provided guidelines for developing and preparing a museum-based essay. As you did in each of the previous chapter skill sets, carefully observe a work chosen from an online site such as those listed on page xiii or from your textbook, and write down everything that you see. Be as thorough as possible, returning to the skills you mastered in the previous chapters. Your list should include both objective data from direct observation and subjective data based on personal assumptions and associations with the work you chose. The combined data (observed and associative) will form the basis of your analytic essay.

Once you have compiled your lists, look through the textbook or online site and observe the works reproduced around the artwork you chose to analyze. How do these works create an environment or a context for the work you studied? The environment may reflect a period (Renaissance, Baroque, Postmodern), an artist (Georgia O'Keeffe, Rachel Ruysch, Artemesia Gentilleschi), a nation (South Africa, France, the United States), or even materials and/or techniques (clay, bronze, printmaking).

However, a museum or gallery environment presents unique experiences that are not available to us when we look at a work of art in a book or online. As suggested earlier in this chapter, as you select a work for your assignment and begin to prepare your lists, carefully observe and record data about the space in which it is displayed, including the theme of the exhibit and surrounding works. As the earlier discussion of shifting meanings of the Igbo sculpture at the Housatonic Museum of Art suggests, the physical environment (a museum or gallery space, an office, a living room, a store-room) can alter the meaning of a work of art. Post-Structuralists call this fluid process of building meanings through shared relationships intertextuality.

Make a list of everything that you see in the presentation space. How are the works arranged? How is the space lit (bright or muted light; general floodlights or dramatic spotlights)? Is the gallery space open or filled? Are the pieces clustered? If so, are they grouped by artist? by school? by theme? Does the title of the show (the theme) suggest that you view the work in a specific way? This is true for both the physical museum and the web museum. Refer to the discussion of the Winslow Homer exhibit in Chapter 2.

If you visit a nonweb-based museum, be aware of how you physically, psychologically, and emotionally relate to both the work that you have chosen to discuss and to the other works in the exhibition space. If the work is large, do you feel overpowered or intimidated by it? If it is a portrait, does the sitter's gaze engage you or do you feel like a voyeur intruding on the sitter's private space? If it is a sculpture, do you feel its presence in the room? Does the sculpture dynamically control the space of the room or is it a passive object?

6
USING THE INTERNET
TO LOOK AT ART

More and more often, students are asked to find images or undertake research projects on the Internet. Most art textbooks now have companion websites that provide study guides, additional images, links to other websites, short videos, and other educational resources that expand the basic narrative of the printed text. This brief chapter presents the virtual museum and image resource sites. A particularly helpful resource is Lois Swan Jones's *Art Information and the Internet* (Oryx Press, 1999), part of a series of resource guides published by Dr. Jones for the Visual Resources Association (VRA) and the Art Libraries Society (ARLIS). The next chapter will discuss online textual resources.

VISITING A VIRTUAL MUSEUM

If you went to a museum website in preparation for your visit, you participated in the recent phenomenon of the virtual museum. The virtual museum is designed to simulate a museum experience without actually entering a bricks-and-mortar structure. The format of the virtual museum varies from institution to institution. Some virtual museums mirror the physical museum, so that we walk through the galleries of the museum on our computer as if we were there.

Others provide images from their collections that can be called up by subject, artist, or media. A new phenomenon is the virtual special exhibit designed exclusively to be seen on the Internet. There are both advantages and disadvantages to the virtual museum.

The image quality of a virtual museum is limited by the resolution of its photographic reproductions. Two common file formats are used to save visual images. The image quality on our screen depends on how the graphic information was initially stored. The graphic interchange format (GIF), a low-resolution file, is commonly used for small or thumbnail images.

Low-resolution images lack clarity, especially if the viewer wants to enlarge them on a monitor to study details. Some image resource sites use GIF files because they are smaller and download more quickly. High-resolution images are stored and transferred through a joint photographic experts group file format (JPEG). These files, in comparison to GIF files, are larger and thus capable of greater clarity in a full screen image. Both file formats use compression algorithms (routines) to make them smaller and more manageable for the web. A JPEG file can be enlarged on computer monitors to study details. To determine how an image was saved, go to the menu bar at the top of the screen. If you are using Netscape as your browser, go to the menu bar View and scroll to Page Info. A two-part information box should come up; the top will include an image list and identify the file format. If your browser is Internet Explorer, go to File and scroll to Properties for the information.

The quality of the image on the monitor is only as good as the resolution of the initial photograph (or scan). The increasing resolution of digital cameras often translates to increased clarity on screen. As in print media, color accuracy is also a concern. Monitors vary in their ability to display color as well. You have experienced this if you have walked through any large electronics store and looked at the banks of monitors on display. Although set to the same programs, there are subtle differences in the color quality of the pictures on screen.

Even with sharp images, however, the physical experience of the work of art is missing when you view it only in a virtual museum. A short movie may allow you to see around a sculpture, but it remains confined within the space of the computer screen. It is not an experience of the space. You may be able to look at Leonardo da Vinci's *Mona Lisa* on the Louvre's website (http://www.louvre.fr/louvrea.htm), but it is not the same thing as visiting her. In this way, the virtual museum has the same limitations as its companion museum catalog.

While the number of images on a virtual museum site is limited, as it is in the physical space of its galleries, links on the websites encourage us to explore a larger field. For example, the Metropolitan Museum of Art in New York (http://www.metmuseum.org/) has more than thirty-five hundred images online from its extensive collection, but with its online links, there are hundreds of thousands of images drawn from around the world. The Louvre in Paris has fifteen hundred pictures and descriptions online according to its website, as well as a Paris Virtual Guide.

COMPASS is the online source for the British Museum (http://www.thebritishmuseum.ac.uk/compass/) with approximately five thousand articles available. Each object in the collection has links, so that we can browse among related objects and research background information about the people and cultures that made or used them. According to the Los Angeles County Museum of Art website (LACMA) (http://www.lacma.org/), eight thousand works from its Asian and Islamic art departments are online, as well as 150,000 publications from the noncirculating art research library. Linked websites such as these often allow the virtual museum visitor to move images located in distant galleries of the museum or in geographically distant museums side-by-side on a computer screen for comparisons among artists or within a single artist's *oeuvre* (work). This is especially easy if you have Internet Explorer as your browser and use the Search function on the Explorer Bar that runs along the edge of the museum home page.

The ability to visit museums and view their collections in distant cities and countries is another advantage of the virtual museum. Although many Western museums have very good collections of Chinese paintings, sculpture, and bronze vessels, Internet access to paintings in the National Palace Museum in Taipei, Taiwan (http://www.huthumble.com/taipai/taipei1.htm) and the Shang and Chou bronze vessels in the Shanghai Museum in China (http://www.sh.com/travel/museum/museum.htm) enriches our understanding of Chinese cultural history. In some cases, museums have objects that are too fragile or too large to be included in traveling exhibitions or are excluded from travel through donation restrictions. Jane Alexander's sculpture *Butcher Boys* (1989) in the National Gallery of South Africa in Cape Town, a monumental work connoting the repressive political climate of South Africa under apartheid, is difficult to transport because of its size (three lifesize polyresin figures seated on a bench). The museum's website (http://www.museums.org.za/sang)

provides access to this image. Increasingly, museums include virtual museum sites to extend their physical exhibition spaces, making works by artists like Alexander available.

While the virtual museum may be the optimal arena for viewing new media works created for viewing on a monitor, many video and digital media artists want the audience to participate in the environment of their display. Nam June Paik (http://www.artincontext.org/artist/p/nam_june_paik/), a pioneer in video art, created wall-sized works that combine multiple monitors. Included in his work and altering the gallery space are soundscapes, projected light from the monitors, and time/motion studies. When we first see his work in a gallery, we may think of commercial television sales and the repetition of imagery in an electronics store. But as we look more closely, Paik's work provokes a series of questions about the function of technology in communication and the confusion of reality with its representation.

LINKING TO A MUSEUM SITE

The following three sites provide links to museums and online galleries. There are many more sites available if you undertake an online search. Make sure that the site you choose is current (go to View on your menu bar and scroll down to Page Info) and that it does not represent a strictly commercial interest (go to the bottom of the webpage to find the creator).

The Virtual Library Museum Pages (VLMP; http://www.icom.org/vlmp/), is maintained by Jonathan Bowen, a Professor of Computing and Information Science at South Bank University in London and supported by the International Council of Museums (ICOM). The site may be entered through a number of mirror sites (a web location that duplicates material on another website) that provide access to VLMP when demand is heavy. VLMP links to museum-related lists, announcements about museum pages, talks on the Virtual Library museum pages, and relevant newsgroup articles.

World Wide Arts Resources can be found at http://wwar.com/. This site, founded by Markus Kruse who holds a Ph.D. in Art Education from Ohio State University is a gateway not only for online information about artists, museums, and galleries but also commercial resources for artists' supplies.

The Museum Computer Network (http://www.mcn.edu/ siteson-line.htm) is guided by a Board of Directors with members drawn from distinguished academic and museum institutions. This networks links museums worldwide and makes their collections available for study.

The Art Museum Image Consortium (AMICO) website (http://www.amico.org) has both public and private online resources. Although the number of images available through this site is substantial, an institution or organization must be a subscriber for you to take advantage of AMICO's resources.

LINKING TO ADDITIONAL DATABASES

The Internet is also the source of online visual resources not connected to museum or gallery collections. Like the museum resources discussed earlier in this chapter, the quality of images may suffer although the quantity of images may be large. If you are using the images for reference or as study aids, the resolution may be sufficient. If you plan to print them for later study, you will be disappointed. Do not expect all the images to be clear or accurate in color and frame. Horizontal images fit more neatly onto a computer screen than do vertical images, so vertical works may be compressed or have an incomplete display. Unless you are familiar with the image, you may not be able to tell if the edges were cropped (cut) to fit the screen. Some useful resources, in addition to the museum and gallery sites discussed above are the Art Index Guide to Asian Art online (http://www.artindex.com/chinese.htm) and Corbis, (http://www.corbis.com/) a private corporation with more than two million images online. Other websites that provide basic information or imagery are the *Artcyclopedia* (http://artcyclopedia.com/index.html) created by John Malyon, to provide references to sites on the World Wide Web where artists' works can be viewed online, and *Art History Resources on the Web* (http://witcombe.sbc.edu/ARTHLinks.html), developed and currently maintained by Chris Witcombe, a professor of art history at Sweet Briar College in Virginia.

DOWNLOADING AND PRINTING IMAGES

Images called up on the web, either through a museum or gallery site or an online image database (repository), can be downloaded into a computer, viewed using a number of graphic applications, and printed. However, the result of this process may yield an image that is significantly inferior to the image on other monitors or display devices.

The computer graphic image on the Internet is the result of many bits of data recorded as pixels (picture elements) and displayed on the horizontal and vertical axes of the monitor. Pixels have no actual dimension, so the quality of a computer graphic depends on the number of pixels in the original graphic file. With fewer bits of information available, the distance between pixels is greater and the clarity of the projected image diminishes. If you look at digital cameras, they are designated as 3.1 Megapixel (a megapixel is one million pixels) (2160 × 1440) or 1.3 Megapixel (1280 × 960). The 2160 × 1440 camera captures more information than the 1280 × 960 camera, yielding a sharper image. Film photographers use the term *resolution* rather than *pixel quality*.

If we increase the size of the image on the monitor beyond its intended resolution (number of available pixels), we see a steplike pixelation of the texture and lines (or edges) and popularly called jaggies; in other words, the resolution of the image suffers. Therefore, a 2160 × 1440 camera produces less pixelation (fewer jaggies) than a 1280 × 960 camera because more primary data yield a sharper final image on a normal display device.

A standard fifteen-inch monitor is approximately 800 × 600 pixels. The following very general rule of thumb can help determine how large to make a display and retain clarity. Multiply the specifications of your monitor by two and do not exceed that number when you zoom in on the screen image. If your initial file is 2160 × 1440, you can safely zoom in twice on an 800 × 600 pixel (fifteen-inch) monitor, but if the file was initially 1280 x 960, you should only zoom in once (and even then there will be some loss of clarity). Cameras designed specifically for Internet applications (webcams) tend to have lower resolution to work compatibly with a standard monitor.

When you print a computer graphic, the printer must interpolate the image and convert it into "dots per inch" (dpi). The print application inserts information based on available data between the pixels to create an image. The greater the initial data (the more pixels of captured information), the greater the clarity of the final printed image.

Copyright law protects computer images, just as it does other information on the computer. Once something is up on the web, it is considered published material. The source and ownership of computer graphics can be traced through their concealed digital watermarks. Always provide the source of your imagery just as you would for any material that you quote in a paper.

CITING DIGITAL INFORMATION

Chapter 7 discusses citation formats for Internet resources. Remember that while you are working actively with a site, you must record its address or URL (uniform resource locator) as it appears in the address bar on the top of your browser screen. Always assume that an Internet image is copyrighted. More rather than less documentation protects you from inadvertent plagiarism.

7
WRITING YOUR ESSAY

You have finished your museum visit, whether actual or virtual, and have notes, a sketch or other reproduction, and memories. Now it is time to sit down and organize an essay. Before you start, review the notes, and add anything that appears to be missing while the experience is fresh in your mind. For review, determine what is most important in your notes and if a theme is evident.

PLANNING YOUR ESSAY

When faced with a writing assignment, many students want to sit down and immediately begin to write. While this may seem to be the most efficient use of your limited time, it is not very practical. A bit of advance planning will produce a finished essay with fewer later revisions.

Before beginning to write, you must define three categories: your subject area, your topic, and your thesis. The *subject area* is the most general of these three requirements; it is the broad category within which you will define your actual topic. If you are asked to "write an essay about Gilbert Stuart's *Athenaeum Portrait of George Washington* (1796)" (Fig. 4), you have been assigned a subject—the Stuart painting. Within this subject area, you will choose a *topic*. The topic of your essay will be an idea within the subject matter that you have been asked to discuss. Within the subject "Gilbert Stuart's portrait of George Washington," you can discuss Stuart as a painter of famous men, Washington as the first president, or the place of the Washington portrait within early American portrait history. From the topic, you will generate a *thesis*.

Your thesis is the specific or central idea you wish to support in your essay. It should be a single, clearly presented assertive statement. It, too, can be the answer to a question addressed to your topic. For example, your answer to the question "What is important about the George Washington portrait?" may be "Washington is a symbol of American nationalism." Your thesis question can be "Why is this Washington portrait a symbol of American nationalism?" You might respond to this question as follows:

> The unassuming candor and absence of political symbols in Gilbert Stuart's portrait of George Washington affirms the principles of a young nation that promoted republican virtues and egalitarian principles over ostentatious wealth and class.

This sentence might be used to initiate writing. It is a very general statement that can provide a starting point for an essay; as you write, it should become more focused and more specific.

UNDERSTANDING THE QUESTION

Before you begin writing your essay, make sure you understand the question. To determine this, highlight some key words.

1. *analyze/analysis*: to break down and examine in detail all components parts.

An analysis involves taking apart and examining a topic to reveal its component parts. By identifying, describing, and questioning all parts of a work (formal elements, design principles, symbols, mythology, and history), we come to a greater appreciation and understanding of the whole. An analysis involves the relationship between *cause and effect*. Any analysis is incomplete, however, without a *synthesis*, the conclusions reached by reassembling the parts back to a meaningful whole.

2.   *argue/argument*: to present material through persuasive reasoning.

Coherent arguments in an essay use factual evidence to support a claim. A good essay also needs a clearly presented point of view or interpretation; a list of facts without an accompanying interpretation is not sufficient to establish a sound argument. Keep in mind that part of your task in arguing a specific point is to convince your reader that your interpretation is the best one available.

3.   *discuss*: to provide meaning to description through illustration and balanced of viewpoints.

A discussion draws on both argument and evaluation in its use of evidence and examples. A good discussion considers many viewpoints before drawing a conclusion.

4.   *assess*: to evaluate or judge something using empirical (observed or measurable) evidence.

To assess the value of a particular problem (perhaps an assigned reading or an historical incident), you need to state your opinion or claim and then provide sound reasons for your position.

5.   *compare/contrast*: to examine one or more objects or theories in order to discover similarities and differences.

A successful comparison contrasts two or more objects, ideas, or theories through careful analysis. Often a professor may ask you to *distinguish* between two theories or events. In this case, you concentrate on their differences and not their similarities.

6.   *deductive/inductive*: two processes of reaching a conclusion. A *deductive* argument moves from the general to the particular; an *inductive* argument moves from particulars to the general.

When you create an inductive conclusion, you generalize because you reach a conclusion based on accumulated particular facts. For example: After finding four fuzzy baby chicks (four particular chicks), I assume that all baby chicks are fuzzy (a generalized statement about chicks). To reach a deductive conclusion, you particularize based on a general rule or set. For example: All baby chicks are fuzzy (a generality); therefore, the next baby chick I see will be fuzzy (a particular chick).

7.   *evaluate*: to describe and assess the worth of something.

To evaluate something, you must first describe it (part of an analysis) and then present a personal viewpoint that establishes its relative value or worth. An assessment without analysis and data is an *opinion* and should be avoided.

INSPIRATION OR PERSPIRATION?

Once the question/assignment is clear, you have been to the museum or gallery and taken careful notes, and you have defined a subject, topic, and thesis, it is time to write. Many students believe in the "light bulb" theory of composition; they sit down and stare at a blank sheet of paper or a blank computer screen until an idea suddenly appears. When lightning does not immediately strike (in the form of a brilliant idea), students become frustrated and discouraged, throw up their hands in disgust, abandon the exercise, or begin to write observations without a thesis.

More often, composing an essay is a laborious process of writing down ideas as they come to you, testing these ideas, and either refining or abandoning them for better ideas focused on the topic. As you write, your central idea will be continually tested, edited, and refined. You may have to discard much of what was originally written. Do not be discouraged; this is a normal part of writing and creates a tighter thesis statement and a better-finished essay.

FREEWRITING

One way to begin the writing process *after* you have determined a broad thesis is to sit down and randomly start writing down ideas as they come to you about your topic or thesis. Keep your notes in front of you as you write. You will see key ideas in your observations drawn from your experience and research. Do not try to edit. Do not be concerned if there are fragments, misspelled words, run-on sentences, or other grammatical problems. This is not a finished work; this is an exercise to help generate ideas. As you brainstorm, build each new sentence on key words from the previous sentence.

Set a time limit; fifteen minutes usually is sufficient for a freewriting session. When your allotted time is up, stop and read what you have written. Is there the kernel of a thesis? Highlight it and then use it as the basis for a second brainstorming session. You may want to do this a number of times. Remember to limit the time of each freewriting session and stay focused.

Freewriting can be especially helpful if you are having trouble finding a topic. Start with the broad subject matter and brainstorm ideas until you find a topic within the subject area. Then take that topic and brainstorm for your thesis.

ORGANIZING AN EFFECTIVE ESSAY

Organization is important in an effective essay. It is important to clearly introduce your topic, and state and support your thesis. If your thesis is very narrow, as it should be for a short essay, you should acknowledge any pertinent facts that you have chosen *not* to discuss so that your reader will not object to their exclusion. Pay particular attention to your opening paragraph. It should not only state your topic and thesis but also suggest the points you propose to cover in the body of the essay. Above all, it should be lively or engaging. A boring introductory paragraph does not encourage your reader to continue reading.

THINKING AND WRITING

If you have taken careful notes on your observations, then your essay is already partially written. Only the organization of the essay itself remains. A thoughtfully chosen topic will focus your analytic essay. A topic for discussion of Andy Warhol's *Brillo Boxes* may be 1950s American consumerism. Your thesis statement should narrowly address the broader question suggested by the topic. A thesis statement within the above topic may focus on Warhol's attitudes toward 1950s consumer culture in the United States. Now begin to describe and discuss the work based on the notes you took at the museum and whatever freewriting you have done. Integrate the material so that it flows well as an essay. At this point, do not make a fact list as if you were writing an encyclopedia. Think of your essay as a formal, polite conversation (formal and polite because you will not use slang or colloquialisms). Do not assume knowledge; expect that your reader is unfamiliar with your subject. Unless your reader has spent as much time as you have looking at and thinking about the artwork on which you are writing, you may, in fact, be more familiar with it. A well-crafted essay moves back and forth between objective (colors, lines, balance, etc.) and subjective (the meanings implied by the colors, lines, balance) discussions. When you feel that you have covered all the points, summarize your topic and thesis.

After you finish writing your essay, read it aloud. This will help to check syntax (word order). If it sounds awkward to your ear, it needs to be rewritten. Always check for typographical errors, spelling errors, and grammatical errors (such as punctuation, agreement, and run-on sentences). While the spellchecker on your computer is helpful, it is not perfect. It can only tell you if a word is properly spelled. However, a properly spelled word may not be the right word to use (for example, there, their, and they're). When a spellchecker corrects a misspelled word, it guesses the word you really want. You must read and check your work carefully.

READING AND REVISING YOUR ESSAY

After you have completed the first draft of your essay, you will need to revise it (Hopefully you have left yourself time to do this!). Ask yourself the following questions:

Topic and Thesis

- Is it interesting to read?
- Is the essay's purpose clear?
- Is the topic narrow enough for the essay?
- Is the thesis statement clear?
- Are the examples relevant and clearly stated?

If you answer "no" to any of these questions, you will need another revision.

Organization

- Is the introduction lively?
- Does each paragraph build from the previous one and develop the thesis?
- Does the conclusion summarize the essay and bring it to a satisfying close?
- Does the body of the essay clearly develop the thesis?

If you answer "no" to any of these questions, you will need another revision.

Writing Style

- Does the essay use both complex and simple sentences?
- Is the vocabulary appropriate?
- Are there slang words ("informal language")?

If you answer "no" to either of the first two questions, or "yes" to the third question, you will need another revision.

Proofreading

- Is the essay free of misspelled words?
- Is the essay free of run-on sentences, fragments, and improper paragraphs?
- Is the punctuation correct?
- Do all subjects (nouns/pronouns) and predicates (verbs) agree?
- Do all nouns and pronouns agree?
- Are any homophonic words (words that sound alike) confused, such as: its/it's, there/their, who's/whose, accept/except, your/you're, to/two/too, affect/effect?

If you answer "no" to any of these questions, or "yes" to the final question, you will need to make corrections. While spellcheckers and grammar checkers can alert you to and help correct some of these problems, the programs are "dumb" and cannot tell you if the right word is in the right place. If you are uncertain when you proofread, give your essay to a friend to check. A fresh pair of eyes may see things you missed.

SOME COMMON MISTAKES

simple/simplistic: Simple is an adjective that indicates a level of complexity; a *simple* solution is modest and direct. A *simplistic* solution is oversimplified and therefore meaningless. It is not a more formal version of the word *simple*.

a lot: These are two separate words, not one. However, this is a colloquialism; it would be better to substitute an adjective such as *many* or a more precise number.

affect/effect: *Affect* is a verb meaning *to influence*. (The rain *affected* my mood.) *Effect* is a noun that indicates a result. (The *effect* of the rain was an abundant crop of weeds.)

accept/except: *Accept* is a verb meaning *to receive*. (Will you *accept* this gift?) *Except* is a verb meaning *to exclude* or *to exempt*.

among/between: Use *among* to compare three or more objects and *between* to compare two objects.

being as/being that: Avoid this construction; use because or structure your sentences to be declarative.

sculpture/sculptor: A *sculptor* is a person who creates a *sculpture*.

its/it's: This is the one exception to the rule about the use of an apostrophe to indicate possession. *Its* is a possessive pronoun; *it's* is a contraction of "it is" or "it has."

their/there: *Their* is a plural possessive pronoun. (This is *their* painting). *There* is a pronoun when used to begin a sentence; the verb following *there* is either singular or plural according to the subject that follows the verb. (*There is* a painting by Anselm Kiefer in the San Francisco Museum of Modern Art. *There are* paintings by Wassily Kandinsky in the Guggenheim Museum.) As an adverb, *there* indicates place. (The photograph by Imogen Cunningham is *there* [as opposed to *here*].)

important/big: *Important* indicates relative worth. Although *big* has assumed the same meaning in everyday conversation as important, its use is improper in an essay. *Big* indicates size, not value.

amount/number: *Amount* indicates volume; *number* indicates quantity. (Meg counted the *number* of paintings in the collection.)

very/way: Although the word *way* has become synonymous with *very* in everyday speech, it is unacceptable in a formal paper.

who/whom/that: If a clause refers back to a human subject, use *who* (subjective pronoun: *Who* is at the door?) or *whom* (objective form of who: To *whom* should I address the letter?); if the clause refers to a nonhuman subject, use *that*.

8

CITING SOURCES
AND RESOURCES

If the visual analysis includes the use of outside resources (perhaps you compared your analysis to another or you researched the history of the artist or the subject), always provide a bibliography or works cited page. If you quote or even *paraphrase* an author's work, you must give that author credit in a footnote (at the bottom of the page) or endnote (at the end of the essay before the works cited page). Passing off another's work as your own is called plagiarism; in most universities, plagiarism can lead to disciplinary action and even dismissal. While ideas considered common knowledge do not have to be cited, if you are in doubt, be safe and acknowledge your source.

If you quote from an outside source, integrate the quotation into your text so that the textual flow is not disrupted. Remember that long quotations (four lines or more) are centered in the text and presented without quotation marks. All quotations are numbered sequentially beginning from the first page of your essay; do not start a new number sequence with each new page.

RESOURCES

Ask your professor about the use of encyclopedias and other general sources. Encyclopedias provide summaries and are not always appropriate for university-level research. However, an exception is the *Grove's Dictionary of Art*, available either online with a password at http://www.groveart.com/ through your school library or in hard copy in the library. Other online resources include *ArtSource* http://www.ilpi.com/artsource/), described on the site as a "gathering point for networked resources on Art and Architecture. The content is selective rather than comprehensive and includes pointers to resources around the net as well as original materials submitted by librarians, artists, and art historians." M. Neil Browne and Stuart Keeley compiled a more complete list of Internet resources in their book *Art on the Internet: Evaluating Online Resources* (Prentice Hall, 2001) as did Barbara Houghton in *The Internet and Art: A Guidebook for Artists* (Prentice Hall, 2002).

Whether you choose online or hardcopy resources, pay close attention to the type and number of sources your professor requires. Generally, sources are described as *primary* (an original text, artwork, book, or article) and *secondary* (a text written about the primary source). For example, *Brillo Box* by Andy Warhol is a primary source (an original sculpture) as are the artist's comments about his work in the *Warhol Diaries*. The New York critic Arthur Danto's text *Beyond the Brillo Box* is a secondary source that discusses the influence of Warhol's sculpture in the art world.

Online resources should be carefully evaluated before citing them because many are not juried before they are posted. In a juried essay, the author or the author's publisher has asked scholars in the discipline to read and comment on the accuracy of the material presented. In a nonjuried essay posted online, there is no scholarly panel to review the material and provide constructive feedback. Look at the webpage address to find the source of the essay. Did it come from a university or museum website? Is it appropriately documented with footnotes and a bibliography? Even this may not provide sufficient information to verify the credibility of the essay; many university classes work on the Internet and post student essays, so you may be looking at work by a student similar to yourself. It will take a bit more research, but one way to confirm the author's status is to search for other examples of the author's work.

If your analysis includes research, you need to carefully document your resources. If you quote or paraphrase something you have read, whether online, in a book, or from a magazine, you must acknowledge the original author, using an appropriate citation.

CREATING FOOTNOTES AND ENDNOTES

Although there are many acceptable forms of documentation, the two most common are the Modern Language Association (MLA) and the *Chicago Manual of Style*. Ask your professor which system is preferred. The *Art Bulletin* of the College Art Association suggests the *Chicago Manual of Style* to its contributors.

You may encounter some difficulties when documenting online resources. The *Chicago Manual of Style* does not yet address formats. However, *The Columbia Guide to Online Style*, edited by Janice Walker and Todd Taylor York (1998), (http://www.columbia.edu/cu/cup/cgos/idx_basic.html) is a good resource, as is the MLA site (*http://www.mla.org*). Many university librarians have placed citation reference guidelines on their university webpages, so check your campus website for information.

MODERN LANGUAGE ASSOCIATION

If you have Internet access, you can go to the MLA website directly by typing http://www.mla.org/; click on MLA style and then click on Documenting from Internet Resources on the sidebar. The MLA online outlines recommended forms for Internet documentation. The following recommendations are taken from the website:

1. provide the Uniform Resource Locator (URL) address
2. provide the date that you accessed the resource parenthesis at the end of your citation
3. provide the name of the list or forum you used for any discussion posting
4. provide the name of a subscription service, if used, and the name of the library webpage used to gain access to that subscription service
5. include the date of the electronic publication or using Show or Page Info on your browser, the date of any modifications or revisions
6. give the name of the compiler or editor who maintains a scholarly site, cited as *Ed. by "Author's First Name" "Author's Surname"*
7. underline the title of a scholarly webpage
8. provide the name of corporate or website name in place of the author if the author's name is unavailable

Remember that the Internet includes scholarly as well as personal documents. Not all Internet materials have been checked for accuracy. There are also many student postings from classes similar to your own. If you use the Internet for research, pay careful attention to who posted the information.

Citation Guidelines for the MLA

The Modern Language Association recommends that a writer provide only the most significant information in-text so that the reader can find the relevant resource in the bibliography or works cited page. Unless the author's name is mentioned in the text or there are multiple works by the same author, the in-text citation includes the author's surname and the page on which the cited material can be found. For example:

> Stated in its simplest terms, the modern curator's job is to take care of the works of art in his department, to display them in a manner best suited to bring out their aesthetic and educational importance, and to advise the trustees regarding new purchases in his field. (Tomkins 229)

Notice that there is no punctuation separating the author's surname from the page number.

> Calvin Tomkins suggests that "the modern curator's job is to take care of the works of art in his department, to display them in a manner best suited to bring out their aesthetic and educational importance, and to advise the trustees regarding new purchases in his field. (229)

Because the author's surname is included in the text, only the page reference is necessary. The same is true if you paraphrase or summarize Tomkins rather than quote verbatim, as in:

> According to Calvin Tomkins, the modern curator is not only a caretaker concerned with maintaining an art collection, but also a consultant to trustees for the acquisition of new works. (229)

If more than one work by Calvin Tomkins is included in the bibliography, then a key word from the title, placed in italics and separated by a comma from the author's surname, should be used. In that case the above citation would look like this:

(Tomkins, *Merchants* 229)

The bibliographic reference for this text looks like this:

Tomkins, Calvin. *Merchants and Masterpieces.* New York: E.P. Dutton & Co., Inc., 1973.

If this was part of a multi-volume work, the volume number would follow the title as: Vol. 1.

Compiling an MLA Bibliography or Works Cited Page

Pay close attention to the punctuation and the use of indentations and follow them exactly. The bibliography or works cited page is not the place for creativity. Works are arranged alphabetically by authors' surnames or by the first word of a title after the article (The, An, A) if there is no author. Titles should be in italics or underlined. The first line is on the outside margin; the second line is indented five spaces. Each entry is double-spaced with double-spaces between entries. A bibliography is never numbered.

Books:

Tomkins, Calvin. *Merchants and Masterpieces.* New York: E.P. Dutton & Co., Inc., 1973.

Edited Anthology:

Benjamin, Walter. "The Work of Art in the Age of Mechanical Reproduction." *Modern Art and Modernism: A Critical Anthology,* Ed. Francis Frascina and Charles Harrison. New York: Harper and Row, 1984. 217-220.

This citation indicates that the editors Frascina and Harrison selected an essay by the German theorist Walter Benjamin for the anthology on modern theory.

Journals:

Levin, G. Roy. "Art Education as Cultural Practice." *The Art Journal* 58.1 (1999): 16-20.

In this entry, 58 indicates the volume and 1 indicates the issue number within volume 58. If the journal is paginated continuously through the entire volume, so that issue two begins numbering where issue one stopped, then only cite the volume number.

Monthly Magazine:

Stone, Laurie. "Holly Hughes: Her Heart Belongs to Daddy." *Ms.* Sept./Oct. 1994:88.

Journals tend to be more scholarly than magazines and the reading public for a journal may be more narrowly defined.

Newspaper Article:

"Sacramento's Poseidon Given New Wardrobe." *San Jose Mercury News* 10 July 2000, 3B+.

Because no author was credited, this article would be alphabetized using the first letter of the first word in the title. This article is found in section B on two separate pages; only indicate the first page and use the plus symbol to indicate multiple pages.

Online Encyclopedia:

"Angelica Kauffmann." http://www.encyclopedia.com/articles/ 06864.html.(6 June 2000).

The Show or Page Info provided no information about either the author or the dates of modification. The date the site is visited is at the end of the citation in parenthesis.

Website:

National Museum of Women in the Arts, Washington, D.C. "Angelica Kauffmann." Mod. 23 Jul 1997. http://www.nmwa. org/legacy/ gallery/g1700s1.html (6 June 2000).

In the above citation, the sponsoring or corporate organization acts as the author, followed by the title of the entry. The date the entry was modified, found in Show or Page Info, follows the title, then the URL address, and finally the date the site was visited.

Webzine (an eZine or online magazine):

"Optical Filters and Digital Cameras." Megapixel.net 3.36 (2001):
15 September 2001. http://www.megapixel.net/html/
issue index.html
The web magazine (or eZine) is a monthly digital camera magazine published only on the web. No author was provided for the article. A web magazine that is also published in a printed format should provide the same information as a print magazine (see above) with the date on access and the URL address at the end.

Weekly Magazine:

Begley, Sharon. "Music and the Brain." *Newsweek* 24 July 2000: 50–
53.

CHICAGO MANUAL OF STYLE

An online guide to the *Chicago Manual of Style Form Guide* can be found at http://www.lib.ohio-state.edu/guides/chicagogd.html. This site was compiled by the Ohio State University Library and is frequently updated. It provides a summary of basic reference formats. Many university librarians have placed summaries of the *Manual*'s guidelines on their websites. Check with your university to see if one is available. If so, follow those guidelines carefully.

Citation Guidelines for the Chicago Manual of Style

Unlike the MLA, the *Chicago Manual of Style* uses footnotes (at the bottom of the page) or endnotes (a separate sheet at the conclusion of the essay) to provide references for quotations, paraphrases, and summaries. A proper footnote for the quotation below is:

> Stated in its simplest terms, the modern curator's job is to take care of the works of art in his department, to display them in a manner best suited to bring out their aesthetic and educational importance, and to advise the trustees regarding new purchases in his field.[1]
> Calvin Tomkins, *Merchants and Masterpieces* (New York: E.P. Dutton & Co., 1973), 229.

The format differs from the bibliography in the use of parenthesis to set off the place of publication, the publisher's name, and the date of publication. If the next quote in your essay is by the same author, then use the Latin abbreviation *Ibid.* If the source is the same but the page is different, then include a new page number, as: *Ibid.*, 230. Some professors prefer that you cite the author's surname, followed by a comma and the page number for subsequent references to a previously cited resource. Consult your instructor. Notice that the number of the footnote is smaller and raised. If you are using a word processor, go to the menu bar (using insert or tools depending on your program) and select footnotes. Follow the writing program's instructions to format your footnote.

Compiling a Bibliography or Works Cited Page Using the *Chicago Manual of Style*

The basic format for bibliographic references is the same in the Chicago style as the MLA. Unlike the MLA, however, entries are single-spaced with double-spacing between entries and the punctuation is different. The *Chicago Manual* has not yet provided a single format for Internet references. Follow the MLA or Columbia guide or ask your instructor. The most important point is to remain consistent in following whatever form you choose.

Books:

Tomkins, Calvin. *Merchants and Masterpieces.* New York: E.P. Dutton & Co., Inc., 1973.

Edited Anthology:

Benjamin, Walter. "The Work of Art in the Age of Mechanical Reproduction." In *Modern Art and Modernism: A Critical Anthology*, edited by Francis Frascina and Charles Harrison. New York: Harper and Row, 1984. 217-220.

Journals:

Levin, G. Roy. "Art Education as Cultural Practice." *The Art Journal* 58 (1999): 16-20.

Monthly Magazine:

Stone, Laurie. "Holly Hughes: Her Heart Belongs to Daddy." *Ms.* Sept./Oct. 1999, 88.

Newspaper Article:

"Sacramento's Poseidon Given New Wardrobe." *San Jose Mercury News* 10 July 2000, sec. B, p.3.

Online Encyclopedia:

"Angelica Kauffmann. "http://www.encyclopedia.com/articles/06864. html (6 June 2000).

The Show or Page Info provided no information about either the author or the dates of modification. The date the site is visited is at the end of the citation in parenthesis.

Website:

National Museum of Women in the Arts, Washington, D.C. "Angelica Kauffmann." Mod. 23 Jul 1997. http://www. nmwa.org/legacy/ gallery/g1700s1.html (6 June 2000).

In the above citation, the sponsoring or corporate organization acts as the author, followed by the title of the entry. The date the entry was modified, found in Show or Page Info, follows the title, then the URL address, and finally the date the site was visited.

Webzine (an eZine or online magazine):

"Optical Filters and Digital Cameras." Megapixel.net 3.36 (2001): 15 September 2001. http://www.megapixel.net/html/issueindex. html.

The web magazine (or eZine) is a monthly digital camera magazine published only on the web. No author was provided for the article. A web magazine that is also published in a printed format should provide the same information as a print magazine (see above) with the date on access and the URL address at the end.

Weekly Magazine:

Begley, Sharon. "Music and the Brain." *Newsweek* 24 July 2000, 50–53.

SUGGESTIONS FOR FURTHER READING

Barnet, Sylvan. *A Short Guide to Writing About Art.* 6th ed. London: Longman, 2000.

Barrett, Terry. *Criticizing Art: Understanding the Contemporary.* 2nd ed. Mountain View, CA: Mayfield Press, 2000.

———. *Criticizing Photography.* Mountain View, CA: Mayfield Press, 2000.

Berger, Arthur Asa. *Seeing is Believing: An Introduction to Visual Communication.* 2nd ed. Mountain View, CA: Mayfield Publishing Co., 1997.

Berger, John. *Ways of Seeing.* London: Penguin, 1977.

Biedermann, Hans. *Cultural Icons & the Meanings behind Them.* Trans. James Hulbert. New York: The Penguin Group/Meridian, 1994.

Browne, M. Neil and Stuart Keeley. *Art on the Internet: Evaluating Online Resources.* Englewood Cliffs, NJ: Prentice Hall, 2001.

Barbara Houghton. *The Internet and Art: A Guidebook for Artists* Engelwood Cliffs, NJ: Prentice Hall, 2002.

Carbone, Nick. *Writing Online: A Student's Guide to the Internet.* Boston: Houghton Mifflin Co., 2000.

Hall, James. *Dictionary of Subjects & Symbols in Art.* New York: Harper & Row, 1979.

Jones, Lois Swan. *Art and Information: How to Find It, How to Use It.* Phoenix, AZ: Oryx Press, 1999.

Pierce, James Smith. *From Abacus to Zeus.* 6th ed. Englewood Cliffs, NJ: Prentice Hall, 2001.

Sayre, Henry. *Writing about Art.* 3rd ed. Englewood Cliffs, NJ: Prentice Hall, 1999.

Sporre, Dennis. *Visual Artsguide.* Englewood Cliffs, NJ: Prentice Hall, 2002.

Taylor, Joshua. *Learning to Look: A Handbook for the Visual Arts.* Chicago: University of Chicago Press, 2000.

Tucker, Amy. *Visual Literacy.* Boston: McGraw-Hill, 2002.

Wink, Richard and Richard Phipps. *The McGraw-Hill Museum-Goer's Guide.* Boston: McGraw-Hill, 2000.

INDEX